Elizabeth Sinkler Coxe's

Tales from the Grand Tour

1890–1910

Women's Diaries and Letters of the South
Carol Bleser, Series Editor

Elizabeth Sinkler Coxe's
Tales
from the
Grand Tour
1890–1910

Edited by Anne Sinkler Whaley LeClercq

University of South Carolina Press

© 2006 University of South Carolina

Published by the University of South Carolina Press
Columbia, South Carolina 29208

www.sc.edu/uscpress

Manufactured in the United States of America

15 14 13 12 11 10 09 08 07 06   10 9 8 7 6 5 4 3 2 1

Library of Congress Cataloging-in-Publication Data

Elizabeth Sinkler Coxe's tales from the grand tour, 1890–1910 / edited by Anne Sinkler
    Whaley LeClercq.
        p. cm. — (Women's diaries and letters of the South)
    Includes bibliographical references and index.
    ISBN-13: 978-1-57003-633-0 (cloth : alk. paper)
    ISBN-10: 1-57003-633-0 (cloth : alk. paper)
        1. Europe—Description and travel. 2. Africa, North—Description and travel.
    3. Coxe, Elizabeth Sinkler, 1843–1919—Travel—Europe. 4. Coxe, Elizabeth Sinkler,
    1843–1919—Travel—Africa, North. I. Coxe, Elizabeth Sinkler, 1843–1919.
    II. LeClercq, Anne Sinkler Whaley, 1942– III. Series.
    D919.E44 2006
    910.4092—dc22   2006006855

Contents

Contents

Illustrations

Series Editor's Preface

Elizabeth Sinkler Coxe's Tales from the Grand Tour, 1890–1910, expertly edited by Anne Sinkler Whaley LeClercq, is the twenty-third volume in what had been the Women's Diaries and Letters of the Nineteenth-Century South series. This series has been redefined and is now titled Women's Diaries and Letters of the South, enabling us to include some remarkably fine works from the twentieth century. This series includes a number of never-before-published diaries, some collections of un-published correspondence, and a few reprints of published diaries—a potpourri of nineteenth-century and, now, twentieth-century Southern women's writings.

The series enables women to speak for themselves, providing readers with a rarely opened window into Southern society before, during, and after the American Civil War and into the twentieth century. The signifi-cance of these letters and journals lies not only in the personal revelations and the writing talent of these women authors but also in the range and versatility of the documents' contents. Taken together, these publications will tell us much about the heyday and the fall of the Cotton Kingdom, the mature years of the "peculiar institution," the war years, the adjustment of the South to a new social order following the defeat of the Confederacy, and the New South of the twentieth century. Through these writings, the reader will also be presented with firsthand accounts of everyday life and social events, courtships and marriages, family life and travels, religion and education, and the life-and-death matters that made up the ordinary and extraordinary world of the American South.

Anne LeClercq has woven together materials from a number of sources to tell a story of a remarkable American woman at the turn of the twen-tieth century. Elizabeth Sinkler Coxe was born on a plantation in South Carolina, grew up during the Civil War, married a northerner, was left a very wealthy widow soon thereafter, and then devoted much of her time and wealth to enjoying the amenities that went with her position. More important, she also devoted much of her time and wealth to the exploration and recovery of ancient Egypt. It is a fascinating story, one well-told. The editor, the great-grandniece of Elizabeth Sinkler Coxe, has worked with family papers to give us an exotic tale redolent of both the last golden years before World War I and of the excitement of the early forays into the ruins of ancient Egypt. The family papers consist of letters from her travels, an unpublished diary kept by a niece who accompanied her on her trips, photographs, sketches, and a typed memoir (the journal) of her travels, which was written during her last years as World War I destroyed forever the world she had so enjoyed.

CAROL BLESER

Other Books in the Series

A Woman Doctor's Civil War:
Esther Hill Hawks' Diary
Edited by Gerald Schwartz

The Letters of a Victorian Madwoman
Edited by John S. Hughes

A Confederate Nurse: The Diary
of Ada W. Bacot, 1860–1863
Edited by Jean V. Berlin

Lucy Breckinridge of Grove Hill: The
Journal of a Virginia Girl, 1862–1864
Edited by Mary D. Robertson

A Northern Woman in the
Plantation South: Letters of Tryphena
Blanche Holder Fox, 1856–1876
Edited by Wilma King

Best Companions: Letters of Eliza
Middleton Fisher and Her Mother,
Mary Hering Middleton, from
Charleston, Philadelphia, and
Newport, 1839–1846
Edited by Eliza Cope Harrison

Stateside Soldier: Life in the Women's
Army Corps, 1944–1945
Aileen Kilgore Henderson

From the Pen of a She-Rebel:
The Civil War Diary of Emilie Riley
McKinley
Edited by Gordon A. Cotton

Between North and South: The Letters
of Emily Wharton Sinkler, 1842–1865
Edited by Anne Sinkler Whaley
LeClercq

A Southern Woman of Letters:
The Correspondence of Augusta
Jane Evans Wilson
Edited by Rebecca Grant Sexton

Southern Women at Vassar:
The Poppenheim Family Letters,
1882–1916
Edited by Joan Marie Johnson

Live Your Own Life: The Family Papers of Mary Bayard Clarke, 1854–1886
Edited by Terrell Armistead Crow and Mary Moulton Barden

The Roman Years of a South Carolina Artist: Caroline Carson's Letters Home, 1872–1892
Edited with an Introduction by William H. Pease and Jane H. Pease

Walking by Faith: The Diary of Angelina Grimké, 1828–1835
Edited by Charles Wilbanks

Country Women Cope with Hard Times: A Collection of Oral Histories
Edited by Melissa Walker

Echoes from a Distant Frontier: The Brown Sisters' Correspondence from Antebellum Florida
Edited by James M. Denham and Keith L. Huneycutt

A Faithful Heart: The Journals of Emmala Reed, 1865 and 1866
Edited by Robert T. Oliver

Preface

Elizabeth Allen Sinkler Coxe lived successfully between North and South during the post–Civil War period, when conflict and animosity still divided the nation. Lizzie, as she was called, was a hybrid, born in 1843 at Belvidere Plantation in Eutawville, South Carolina, but her mother, Emily Wharton Sinkler, and her mother's parents, the Whartons, were from Philadelphia. She overcame the emotional trauma of the Civil War. Despite growing up in antebellum South Carolina, she married a Union army major from Philadelphia and moved with him to coal-mining country in Drifton, Pennsylvania. Lizzie had been married only three years when her thirty-year-old husband, Charles Brinton Coxe, died in Egypt on January 3, 1873, leaving her a widow at the age of twenty-nine with a young son, Eckley Brinton Coxe Jr. Lizzie showed poise, determination, and courage in the face of this adversity. She moved vigorously into a new phase of her life, one centered on Drifton, Philadelphia, and the world. She and her son, Eckley Jr., built a magnificent house in Drifton and became active members of this tiny coal town that was the home of her Coxe in-laws. She immersed herself in the cultural world of Philadelphia, taking particular interest in music and the archaeological works of the University of Pennsylvania. She fulfilled a lifelong passion for exploration, spending almost five months of each year traveling across Europe and Asia.

The end of the nineteenth century was the period of great power hegemony, when France, England, and Germany developed protectorates from Egypt and the Sudan to Algeria. Lizzie and her son, Eckley, traveled through the vast reaches of this stately Old World empire, from Madeira to Khartum. She was undeterred by the exigencies of steamships, trains, horses, buggies, heat, long skirts, and the other difficulties of travel.

Lizzie's other great passions were her son and her extended family. She became the surrogate mother for all her young Southern nieces and nephews. She was determined that they not be left behind in a rural, under-educated South, increasingly mired in poverty and racial conflict. She always invited several of these nieces along on her travels, making sure that they met the eligible and attractive young of Europe. These wonderful excursions became a legend in the Sinkler family, with many tales of adventurous trips to Egypt, Turkey, France, Italy, and Greece. Lizzie traveled in style, staying in elegant hotels and carrying her personal servants on each trip. Despite such luxuries, conditions were often primitive, and explorations were made on donkey, on camel, and on foot. Lizzie was a devoted and adoring mother. Her son was her constant companion, and his interests became her interests.

Lizzie was my great-grandaunt. I grew up hearing stories from my great-aunts and my grandmother of their wonderful excursions abroad before the Old World order was changed irretrievably by the physical and cultural destruction of World War I. I learned of Lizzie's youth through my research on her mother, Emily Wharton Sinkler. Lizzie's young life and exploits are an intimate part of both *An Antebellum Plantation Household* and *Between North and South,* my two earlier works.[1]

Lizzie grew up in a world where letter writing was integral to communication. Women spent a part of every day writing letters to keep far-flung family and friends together. In 1998 I became the owner of Lizzie's journals describing her journeys abroad. She had apparently written these accounts between 1916 and 1919. They are in typed format with her handwritten corrections. In 1999 I was given a trove of Lizzie's letters with firsthand accounts of her excursions. In addition, in 1912 Lizzie had privately published *Memories of a South Carolina Plantation during the War.* It was based on a diary she kept at Belvidere during the Civil War.

These various primary documents provide firsthand accounts of American Victorian life in the late nineteenth century. Lizzie's story is imbued with qualities that are still of value today. She had a sense of adventure. She was open to a world of new cultures and different places. She thrilled to

---

1. Anne Sinkler Whaley LeClercq, *An Antebellum Plantation Household, Including the South Carolina Low Country Receipts and Remedies of Emily Wharton Sinkler* (Columbia: University of South Carolina Press, 1996). *Between North and South: The Letters of Emily Wharton Sinkler, 1842–1865* (Columbia: University of South Carolina Press, 2001).

the beauty of sunrise over the Nile or a gift of wildflowers; she especially loved lilies and violets. She was an adoring mother and aunt, guiding her son, her nieces, and nephews in the intricacies of manners and customs. She and her son, Eckley, were generous with their wealth, sharing their resources with family and with the University of Pennsylvania. Her story provides insight into many facets of late nineteenth century life.

I am indebted to Elizabeth Connor, a superior librarian and superb research assistant who has assisted me in locating important facts, in writing and editing, and in ascertaining genealogical connections that would otherwise have remained unearthed. I owe a special acknowledgement for the contributions of Carol Bleser, professor emerita of history at Clemson University and general editor of the Women's Diaries and Letters of the South publication series. This book finds excellent companions in the series. Dr. Bleser made contributions to the final text, one of the most important being her recommendations that I emphasize the relationships between the Coxe and Middleton families, especially the families' interactions with Elizabeth Sinkler Coxe. She helped settle my perspective that Elizabeth was a southern lady with a strong and supportive northern family. In addition Alexander Moore, acquisitions editor at the University of South Carolina Press, provided advice respecting editorial choices to make and offered insights into the intellectual climate of turn-of-the-century America. These two scholars are both historians and documentary editors. Their counsel has been much appreciated. Finally Alessandro Pezzati, archivist of the University of Pennsylvania Museum, has been of particular assistance in providing access to the Eckley B. Coxe Jr. Collections of the museum and also in providing photographs from the Museum Collections.

The book is dedicated to my three sons, Frederic Theodore LeClercq, Ben Whaley LeClercq, and William Kershaw Fishburne LeClercq. Each has inherited Lizzie's zest for the untried and unknown, and each has spent considerable time exploring the world.

Editorial Note

The diaries, letters, and business documents of Elizabeth Sinkler Coxe (1843–1919) and Eckley Brinton Coxe Jr. (1872–1916) provide significant primary material relating to the discovery of Pharaonic Egypt by the West in the years 1890–1917. Elizabeth and Eckley had multiple reasons for sponsoring the University of Pennsylvania archaeology excavations in Egypt from 1905 to 1917. A January visit to Egypt with its dry warm climate was seen as an antidote for many ailments from tuberculosis to cancer. Christians of all denominations hoped that the early truths of Christianity might be revealed in finding the biblical Moses and his escape from Egyptian tyranny. The French invasion of Egypt in 1797 and the discovery and deciphering of the Rosetta Stone by Champollion unlocked a frenzy of European and American interest in ancient Egypt. Each of these motivated their travels.

Elizabeth documented each of her yearly trips from 1890 forward with a travel diary, which she saved in typed format. Those travel diaries are reproduced exactly as she wrote them without changes in spelling or corrections. She also wrote her family on hotel stationery, and these letters likewise have been reproduced exactly as she wrote them. The diaries and letters have been amplified with footnotes from sources contemporaneous with Elizabeth's travels, such as Baedekers or Cooks travel guides. Changes in spelling from her day to the present have been noted, such as Aswan (today) for Assouan (her day), or Khartum (today) for Khartoum (her day). Much has been uncovered both in Egyptian history and archaeology since 1917. Where appropriate this knowledge has been included.

Elizabeth's knowledge was that of a seasoned traveler with an appreciation for archaeology. However, her insights were enriched by an active association with individuals from the University of Pennsylvania Museum, such as David Randall MacIver, the chief curator for the museum's archaeological digs in Buhen, in Upper Nubia, and the assistant curator, Leonard Woolley. In addition Elizabeth was an active reader, with the most important histories of Egypt and the Sudan in her personal library. Her collection included many volumes, three of which this author inherited. They are Robert Hichens, *Egypt and Its Monuments* (New York: Century, 1908); James Henry Breasted, *A History of Egypt* (New York: Charles Scribner's Sons, 1911); and Rudolf C. Slatin Pasha, *Fire and Sword in the Sudan* (London: Edward Arnold, 1896). In addition Elizabeth learned from her son, Eckley Brinton Coxe Jr., who served as chairman of the museum board of the University of Pennsylvania. He funded the museum's expeditions to Egypt and Nubia and arranged and paid for the return shipments, bringing back to the museum the largest sphinx ever shipped until that time. Elizabeth was a "Sunday artist" and a lover of poetry. She combined the two, illustrating her enjoyment of her trips with scenes from her journeys. Those paintings and poetry are reproduced here. Some of her trips were also documented by photography and are used here as illustrations.

The original documents and illustrative materials texts that comprise this work are among a large collection of Sinkler and related family papers in possession of the editor. The published text combines transcribed original holograph letters and a series of typescript "recollections" that Elizabeth Sinkler Coxe prepared during 1916 and 1917. Lizzie Coxe wrote out her recollections in longhand, and then she or another person created typescripts. Lizzie read through the typescripts, making handwritten additions and corrections. The recollections are in diary form, allowing convenient interpolation of the transcribed letters, without interfering with the chronological organization of the text. There is some duplication in the narrative when recollections reprise events mentioned in the letters. These duplications—for example, the tale of the Arab boy who carried oranges and a mummy skull in his robe and the 1895 Shepheard's Hotel letter—offer insights into the way Lizzie composed her recollections and give the reader confidence in the strength of her memory.

Identification of People

Coxe, Charles Brinton, Sr. (February 4, 1843–January 3, 1873). Charles Brinton Coxe was the son of Charles Sidney Coxe (1791–1879) and Anna Maria Brinton (1801–1876), cousin of George Brinton McClellan (1826–1885), and grandson of Tench Coxe (1755–1824). Charles's third cousin was Edward Robbins Wharton.[1] Charles was a scholar, having taken the highest rank in the University of Pennsylvania class of 1862. He served in the Union Cavalry from 1862 to 1865, rising to the rank of major of the Sixth Pennsylvania Cavalry, Rush's Lancers,[2] the only lancer regiment in the Union Cavalry. After he was discharged from the army on June 17, 1865, he joined Coxe Brothers & Company in Hazelton, Pennsylvania, along with his brothers Eckley Brinton Coxe, Alexander "Aleck" Brinton Coxe, Henry Brinton Coxe, and Brinton Coxe, and cousin Franklin Coxe. Charles married Elizabeth Sinkler on June 14, 1870. The Coxe family was a distinguished, old Philadelphia family and were lifetime friends of Lizzie's grandparents, Thomas Isaac Wharton[3] and Arabella Griffith Wharton.

    1. Edward Robbins Wharton (1850–1928) was the former husband of Edith Newbold Jones Wharton (1862–1937), the renowned writer (see Louis Auchincloss, *The Vanderbilt Era: Profiles of a Gilded Age* [New York: Charles Scribner's Sons, 1989]).
    2. Eric J. Wittenberg's book about the Union cavalry quotes Lt. Charles Coxe's comment in an 1863 letter to John Cadwalader: "Raids are grand humbugs" (*The Union Cavalry Comes of Age: Hartwood Church to Brandy Station, 1863* [Washington, D.C.: Brassey's, 2003], 232). Coxe served in the 6th Pennsylvania Cavalry (also known as the 70th Regiment of Pennsylvania Volunteers), which was commanded by Col. Richard Henry Rush (1825–1893), great-grandson of noted Philadelphia physician Benjamin Rush (1745–1813). Col. Rush armed his regiment with lances, hence the name "Rush's Lancers" (100, 137).
    3. Thomas Isaac Wharton was a first cousin to William Wharton (1790–1856), who was the father of Joseph Wharton (1826–1909), the renowned manufacturer,

Coxe, Charles Sidney (1791–1879). Son of Tench Coxe (1755–1824) and Anna Maria Brinton (1801–1876), Charles Sidney Coxe served as the executor of his grandfather's estate and as early as 1854 leased land to other companies to establish coal mines near present-day Eckley, about three miles from Drifton, Pennsylvania. Recognizing the difficulties inherent in mining coal, transporting it, and taking it to market, Charles Sidney Coxe encouraged his own sons to focus on education, an emphasis that led his son Eckley to graduate from the University of Pennsylvania and to obtain a first-rate mining education in Europe while son Aleck studied at the University of Pennsylvania.[4] Charles Sidney Coxe's sons and a nephew established Coxe Brothers & Company on January 30, 1865.[5] Charles Sidney Coxe died in Drifton on November 19, 1879.

Coxe, Eckley Brinton, Sr. (June 4, 1839–May 13, 1895). Eckley Brinton Coxe was the son of Charles Sidney Coxe (1791–1879) and Anna Maria Brinton (1801–1876), cousin of George B. McClellan (1826–1885), and grandson of Tench Coxe (1755–1824). The name Eckley comes from Sarah Eckley (1690–1725), Tench Coxe's grandmother. Eckley Sr.'s grandfather, Tench Coxe, had the astuteness and vision to retain land acquired by his grandfather, Daniel Coxe (1673–1739), to acquire more land, and to form a company that profited from the mining of anthracite. As early as 1794,

---

metallurgist, nickel monopolist, and philanthropist. Joseph Wharton helped found Swarthmore College and donated generously to the University of Pennsylvania. Wharton's largesse helped establish the Wharton School of Finance and Commerce ("Joseph Wharton," *Dictionary of American Biography,* Base Set, American Council of Learned Societies, 1928–36; reproduced in *Biography Resource Center* [Farmington Hills: Gale Group, 2004], http://galenet.galegroup.com/servlet/BioRC [accessed July 12, 2005]). Wharton's nickel mine was located about ninety miles south of Drifton, in Gap, Pennsylvania (Joseph Wharton Family Papers, 1691–1955, Friends Historical Library of Swarthmore College, http://www.swarthmore .edu/Library/friends/ead/5162jowh.htm [accessed July 13, 2005]).

4. "Background Note," Sophia Yarnall Jacobs Papers, 1861–1990, http://www2 .hsp.org/collections/manuscripts/j/jacobs3007.htm (accessed July 12, 2005). Coxe Brothers & Co. "shipped their first coal" in June 1865 (H. C. Bradsby, ed., *History of Luzerne County Pennsylvania* [Chicago: S. B. Nelson, 1893], http://www.rootsweb.com/~usgenweb/pa/luzerne/1893hist/ch11.htm [accessed July 12, 2005]).

5. Bradsby, ed., *History of Luzerne County Pennsylvania.*

Tench Coxe stated: "All of our coal has hitherto been accidentally found on the surface of the earth or discovered in the digging of common cellars or wells; so that when our wood-fuel shall become scarce, and the European methods of boring shall be skillfully pursued, there can be no doubt of our finding it in many other places."[6]

Coxe family members settled in Beaver Meadow, an anthracite region in Carbon County, Pennsylvania, in the early 1820s, and relocated to Drifton, about seven miles north in Luzerne County, after the Civil War. Tench's grandsons (Charles Brinton Coxe, Eckley Brinton Coxe, Alexander "Aleck" Brinton Coxe, Henry Brinton Coxe, Brinton Coxe, and Franklin Coxe) formed Coxe Brothers & Company in Pennsylvania's Lehigh region (Carbon, Luzerne, and Schuylkill counties) and built their fortunes from leasing land and later operating coal mines.[7] Later on, more relatives joined the company, including cousin Arthur McClellan (1839–1904), who died in Drifton. Eckley Sr. ("Eck") founded the Industrial School for Miners and Mechanics[8] in 1879 and held leadership positions in a number of engineering societies, including the American Society of Civil Engineers, the Institute of Mechanical Engineers, and the American Institute of Mining Engineers. In 1880 he was elected to Pennsylvania's state senate, was reelected in 1881, and later "resigned . . . because he would not swear he had spent no money to get it."[9] By the end of his life, Eck was credited with more than one hundred patents, many related to mechanical stoking,[10]

6. Tench Coxe, *A View of the United States of America* (Philadelphia, 1794).

7. Tench Coxe's grandchildren "leased the Drifton Property from their grandfather's estate and formed Coxe Brothers and Company" (Coxe Family Mining Papers—The Companies, Historical Society of Pennsylvania,http://www2.hsp.org/collections/coxe/company.html [accessed June 23, 2005]).

8. This school has changed names several times since its founding and is now known as MMI (Mining and Mechanical Institute) Preparatory School. The school originally taught "basic math, science, and English" to miners ("Shop Talk," *Progressive Engineer*, April/May 2002, http://www.progressiveengineer.com/ [accessed July 12, 2005]).

9. "Eckley B. Coxe Is Dead: Was the Largest Individual Coal Operator in the Country," *New York Times*, May 14, 1895.

10. "Eckley Brinton Coxe," *Dictionary of American Biography*, Base Set, American Council of Learned Societies, 1928–36; reproduced in *Biography Resource Center* [Farmington Hills: Gale Group, 2004], http://galenet.galegroup.com/servlet/BioRC [accessed July 12, 2005].

which optimized fuel efficiency and performance of locomotive engines. Eck and Sophia had no children of their own but were close to Charles and Lizzie Coxe's son, Eck, known as Eck Jr. in an effort to distinguish him from his uncle.

Coxe, Eckley Brinton, Jr. (May 31, 1872–September 21, 1916). Known as Eck Jr., he was the son of Elizabeth Sinkler (1843–1919) and Charles Brinton Coxe (1843–1873). He inherited great wealth from his father, Charles Brinton Coxe, and from his uncle Eckley Brinton Coxe (1839–1895),[11] who had made a fortune in anthracite coal mining. Eck Jr. devoted himself to Egyptian archaeology in the memory of his father and served as the president of the museum board and chief financial supporter of the University of Pennsylvania Museum and its fieldwork program in Egypt. Beginning in 1907, he funded excavations to a number of sites in Egypt and Nubia, including famous ancient cities such as Dendera, Giza, and Memphis. Under his patronage, the museum undertook the first scientific exploration of Nubia, discovering the oldest piece of worked iron in existence, dating back to 2000 B.C.E. He funded the expedition of 1915 at Memphis that revealed the temple and throne room of Merenptah, who some scholars identify with the Pharaoh of the Exodus. Eckley's portrait was painted with a small black statuette of Merer, the Gardener. A May 22, 1916, newspaper account describes the expedition's discovery of an ancient palace next to the Temple of Moses.[12] He was known for his fine stewardship and generosity, leaving the museum over five hundred thousand dollars after he died in September 1916. Eck Jr. was devoted throughout his life to his mother. Together they built their beautiful and beloved home, Windy Hill, in Drifton, Pennsylvania, northwest of Philadelphia and south of Wilkes-Barre.

11. Although a nephew with the same name as the uncle is not usually known as Junior, in this case it is believed that young Eckley called himself Junior as an indicator of his great respect for his uncle Eckley and to distinguish the careers of each.

12. "Discovers Ancient Palace: Excavated on the Nile by Dr. Fisher of Coxe Expedition," *New York Times,* May 22, 1916. This brief account mentions Clarence W. Fisher, director of the Eckley B. Coxe Jr. expedition, who in fact was Clarence Stanley Fisher (1876–1941), a renowned archaeologist, unrelated to the Coxe family's Fisher relatives but instrumental in Coxe expeditions.

Coxe, Elizabeth Allen Sinkler (July 7, 1843–October 24, 1919). Known as
Lizzie, Elizabeth Allen Sinkler was Emily Wharton and Charles Sinkler's
oldest child. On June 14, 1870, she married Charles Brinton Coxe of Drifton and Philadelphia, Pennsylvania. Charles died on January 3, 1873, in
Cairo, Egypt. Their first child, Charles Jr., died in infancy, and their second
son, Eckley Brinton Coxe (Eck), was born on May 31, 1872. Lizzie became
the surrogate mother of her brothers and sisters after Emily Sinkler's un-
timely death on February 10, 1875. Lizzie and Caroline, her youngest sister (nicknamed Carrie), became inseparable friends, living together at a
shared house at 1604 Locust Street in Philadelphia. In 1895, Lizzie and Eck
built a forty-eight-room mansion called Windy Hill in Drifton,[13] Pennsylvania. Each year Lizzie traveled to Europe on the "grand tour" and brought
along her Southern nieces (Charles and Anne Porcher Sinkler's three girls,
Emily, Anne, and Caroline; and Mary Wharton Sinkler and Charles
Stevens's two girls, Elizabeth and Laura) with her to Rome, Genoa, Naples,
Athens, Constantinople, Cairo, Luxor, and other great cities on the tour.
Lizzie chronicled her adventures in Egypt and Europe in several short es-
says as well as in letters home to her Southern family. These are published
here for the first time.

Coxe, Sophia G. (November 24, 1841–March 1, 1926). Sophia (sometimes
called Sophy or Toty)[14] was the daughter of Joshua Francis Fisher (1807–
1873) of Philadelphia and Elizabeth Izard Middleton (1815–1890) of

13. According to the June 1880 census, several Coxe sisters, brothers, and their
wives lived next door to one another in Drifton, Pennsylvania. The dwelling occupied by Rebecca Coxe (1834–1910) was shared with her sister Anna B. and a number of servants. Next door lived Alexander Coxe, his wife Sophia E., son Daniel,
daughter Anna B., two nephews, and servants. Eckley B. Coxe Sr. and his wife
Sophia G. and two servants lived in the next house. Elizabeth Coxe and her young
son Eckley B. Jr. lived in the following house with three servants (Census Office.
Tenth Decennial Census, 1880, http://ancestry.com/ [accessed June 27, 2005]).
Anna Sophia Yarnall Jacobs (1902–1993), granddaughter of Alexander "Aleck"
Brinton Coxe, wrote a fictional account of the Coxe family, which was entitled *The
Clark Inheritance* (New York: Walker, 1981). Most of the book's drama surrounds
the careers and lives of Eckley Brinton Coxe Sr. and the Jacobs' grandfather Alex-
ander Brinton Coxe.
14. As a young child Sophia was called "Toty" by her mother, Eliza Middleton
Fisher (Eliza Cope Harrison, *Best Companions: Letters of Eliza Middleton Fisher and*

Charleston, South Carolina. Sophia married Eckley Brinton Coxe (1839–1895) in 1868 and relocated to Drifton, Pennsylvania. While her sister-in-law Lizzie Sinkler Coxe traveled the world, Sophia tended to the poor, earning the sobriquet "Angel of the Coalfields." Despite Sophia's grand upbringing, life was rather austere in their Drifton home, which resembled a farmhouse rather than a mansion.[15] Sophia's brother-in-law, Alexander Brinton Coxe, was married to Sophia Eliza Norris. Interestingly, Sophia's sister Maria Middleton Fisher (1847–1933) married another Coxe brother, constitutional law expert Brinton Coxe (1833–1892), and also lived in Drifton. Family friend of the Coxes, particularly of Charles Brinton Coxe, and the Fishers, John Cadwalader (1843–1925) married another sister in the same family, Mary Helen Fisher (1844–1937), whose daughter Sophia (Sophy) Cadwalader (1867–1955) later traveled with Elizabeth Sinkler. Sophy edited a memoir of her grandfather titled *Recollections of Joshua Francis Fisher Written in 1864*, published by D. B. Updike and the Merrymount Press.

Fishburne, Anne Wickham Sinkler (November 4, 1886–January 1, 1983). The daughter of Charles St. George Sinkler and Anne Wickham Porcher Sinkler, Anne was a favorite niece of Elizabeth Allen Sinkler Coxe. Anne traveled with Lizzie on the 1910 Orient Express trip described in this book and on many other expeditions. She married William Kershaw Fishburne, a Berkeley County, South Carolina, public-health doctor on April 14, 1910. Her book *Belvidere*, published by the University of South Carolina Press in 1942, described life on the family plantation in fine detail.[16]

Manning, Elizabeth Allen Sinkler (September 16, 1821–April 2, 1908). Lizzie was named for her aunt Elizabeth Allen Sinkler, and she spent time with her in the Sand Hills. Eliza was the only daughter of Elizabeth Allen Broun (1784–1824) and William Sinkler (1787–1853). She lived at Eutaw Plantation with her four brothers, James Sinkler (1810–1854), Charles

---

Her Mother, Mary Hering Middleton, from Charleston, Philadelphia, and Newport, 1839–1846 [Columbia: University of South Carolina Press, 2001]).

15. James J. Bohning, "Angel of the Anthracite: The Philanthropic Legacy of Sophia Georgina Coxe," *Canal History and Technology Proceedings* (2005): 155.

16. Anne Sinkler Fishburne, *Belvidere: A Plantation Memory* (Columbia: University of South Carolina Press, 1950).

Sinkler (1818–1894), Seaman Deas Sinkler (1816–1847), and William Henry Sinkler (1820–1856). Eliza married Richard Irvine Manning II (1817–1861) of Sumter District on March 3, 1845. She was a tiny woman who wore a size three-and-a-half shoe. Her husband acquired forty-one hundred acres near Manchester, Clarendon, Sumter District, and named their house Homesley. This was in the famed Santee High Hills. Richard and Eliza had a total of seven children, three of whom died as infants. When the Civil War began in 1860, although Richard Manning opposed secession, he raised and equipped an infantry company known as the Manning Guards at his own expense. His younger brother, Brown,[17] led the guards as captain. Richard Manning died at his home of typhus fever in October 1861, leaving Eliza to manage his estate and raise their children. Eliza was a tower of strength to her family during the Civil War[18] and persevered to preserve and educate her family after the war. Eliza's daughter Elizabeth Allen Sinkler Richardson characterized her mother as "brave and noble," recalling lovingly: "My Mother's home 'Homesley' was indeed the home for all. . . . My mother was a very remarkable woman; for though

17. Brown Manning (1824–1881) was inducted as a first lieutenant into Company C of the Confederate Army, served as a captain in Company C of the infantry regiment of the Hampton Legion, and was discharged as an aide-de-camp to Company F of the 1st Regiment of the Mobile Volunteers Alabama (United States National Archives, *Civil War Compiled Military Service Records* [Provo, Utah: Ancestry.com, 1999– , database online at http://ancestry.com, accessed December 1, 2005). Brown Manning was the son of Richard Irvine Manning (1789–1836) and Elizabeth Peyre Richardson (1794–1873) and married Elizabeth Gabriella Boykin (1847–1924), daughter of Alexander Hamilton Boykin Sr. and Sarah Jones DeSaussure. Brown's siblings include Richard Irvine Manning II (1817–1861), who married Elizabeth Allen Sinkler (1821–1908), and John Laurence Manning (1816–1889), who married Susan Frances Hampton (1816–1845), daughter of Wade Hampton. John Laurence Manning later married Sallie Bland Clarke. When Brown Manning was imprisoned at Johnson's Island, Ohio, he wrote to his uncle Henry Wharton several times in May 1865 requesting funds to purchase prison food and to leave Ohio, travel to New York, and then home to South Carolina (Sinkler Family Papers 1742–1962, 1100.00, South Carolina Historical Society, Charleston).

18. Robert Milton Burts, *Richard Irvine Manning and the Progressive Movement in South Carolina* (Columbia: University of South Carolina Press, 1974), 4.

my two Uncles and their families and my grandmother and aunt all lived with her, there was never any unpleasantness and all went smoothly."[19]

Manning, Laura Ann Stevens (September 11, 1889–March 31, 1988). Laura was one of Lizzie Sinkler Coxe's many nieces. She went on several of the trips to Europe with Lizzie and Eck, including the trip on the Orient Express to Constantinople, and also several of the Egyptian expeditions. She was the daughter of Mary Wharton Sinkler Stevens (1857–1934), Lizzie's younger sister. Laura was to marry Wyndham Manning (1890–1967), her cousin, and live in Columbia, South Carolina. Known as Baby, she was a lady of great strength, moral conviction, and determination. She had a beautiful carriage, and all five feet and ten inches of her strong frame moved with grace and dignity.

Martin, Elizabeth Allen Stevens (December 31, 1884–March 15, 1973). Known as Liz, she often accompanied Lizzie on her journeys abroad. She was the daughter of Mary Wharton Sinkler Stevens (1857–1934), Lizzie's younger sister. She married Alexander "Alec" Martin (1881–1932) and lived in Charleston, South Carolina, at their lovely home on Rainbow Row. She was a charming hostess, often opening her home and garden to her friends and great-nieces.

Porcher, Julius Theodore, M.D. (April 1, 1829–November 25, 1863). Julius Porcher was the son of Dr. Thomas William Porcher (1807–1889) of Walworth[20] and Ellinor Cordes Gaillard. When Julius married Mary Fanning Wickham[21] of Virginia, his wedding present from his father was St. Juliens Plantation, just west of Eutawville. The lovely oak-lined entrance comes up from the River Road in the shape of a J. The black Italian marble mantels in the living room were brought back from Italy by Julius Porcher, who

19. Elizabeth Sinkler Richardson, "Recollections," a four-page, undated typewritten document in the possession of author LeClercq.

20. According to MacDowell, "Walworth was named by Major Porcher in affectionate rememberance [*sic*] of the village near London where he had been educated" (Dorothy Kelly MacDowell, comp., *Gaillard Genealogy: Descendants of Joachim Gaillard and Esther Paparel* [Columbia, S.C.: R. L. Bryan, 1974], 244).

21. Mary Fanning Wickham (1831–1875) was the daughter of Edward Fanning Wickham and Lucy Carter; a cousin of Williams Carter Wickham (1820–1888), a Confederate general; and a distant cousin of Gen. Robert E. Lee (1807–1870).

had studied medicine in Paris. Julius and Mary Wickham Porcher's daughter, Anne Wickham Porcher (1860–1919), Lizzie's sister-in-law, who was raised in New York City, was to marry Charles and Emily Sinkler's youngest son, Charles St. George Sinkler (1853–1934). It was Charles and Anne's daughters, Emily and Anne, who traveled extensively with Lizzie and Eck.

Roosevelt, Emily Wharton Sinkler (October 23, 1884–April 20, 1970). "Em," as she was known, was a devoted niece of Lizzie Sinkler Coxe. She was the oldest daughter of Charles St. George Sinkler (1853–1934) and Anne Wickham Porcher (1860–1919). Em traveled on most of Lizzie and Eck's Egyptian expeditions, leaving friends and admirers in her wake. She was to marry Nicholas Guy Roosevelt (1883–1965) and live, like her Aunt Lizzie, between North and South. Her homes were at the Highlands in Ambler, Pennsylvania, and at Gippy Plantation near Moncks Corner, South Carolina, where she and her husband raised a prime herd of Guernsey milk cows. She was a great patron of music and the arts.

Sinkler, Anna Linton Thomson (November 5, 1823–November 9, 1873). Anna was married to Charles Sinkler's younger brother and her own first cousin, William Henry Sinkler (1820–1856), on March 4, 1847. She was Lizzie's aunt. She had a beautiful voice, and together Emily Sinkler and Anna put on many performances at Eutaw and Belvidere. Anna Linton Thomson Sinkler wrote in her unpublished history of the Sinkler family:

> After James' death his widow Margaret Cantey [Sinkler] built Belvidere and moved up there early in 1800. Her daughter Margaret Anna was married there to John Linton Thomson Dec. 17, 1816, by the Rev. Charles Snowden. John Linton and Margaret Anna [Sinkler] Thomson had two daughters, Margaret Cantey and Anna Linton. The parents died when they were very young and their Uncle William Sinkler was their guardian. They were sent to Madame Talvande's school in Philadelphia when very young and Anna became an accomplished French scholar and had a beautiful voice. . . . Anna had a magnificent contralto voice. Emily Wharton also had a beautiful voice and when they were all living at Eutaw, Uncle Mazyck Porcher who lived at Mexico plantation fifteen miles down the River Road often used to drive up and spend the evening just to hear them sing.[22]

22. Anna Linton Sinkler, "A History of the Sinkler Family," unpublished manuscript in the possession of author LeClercq.

Anna and Emily Wharton Sinkler were inseparable friends. She was described by Elizabeth Allen Sinkler Richardson: "Some of the happiest days of my life were spent with my Aunt, Mrs. William Sinkler [Anna Linton]. One of the loveliest women, possessed of a wonderful voice whose rich and mellow notes sank into your heart; and she and my aunt, Mrs. Charles Sinkler [Emily] with whom I also spent many happy days, used to sing many lovely duets. Aunt Anna's house . . . was always open to her friends and she was always in the midst of them, making herself one of them. Many happy days were spent with my Uncle and Aunt Mr. & Mrs. Charles Sinkler, and the intimacy begun in childhood has ripened into lasting friendship."[23]

Sinkler, Caroline Sidney (April 23, 1860–1948). Carrie, as she was affectionately called, was Lizzie's sister and traveling companion. She was the youngest child of Emily and Charles Sinkler. She had three splendid homes, the Highlands in Ambler, Pennsylvania, 1604 Locust Street in Philadelphia, and a cultural Mecca, "Wrong Roof" on the Eastern Shore at Gloucester, Massachusetts. She became a great patron of young artists and was a much beloved dowager. Caroline was engaged to marry Philadelphia architect John Stewardson (1858–1896), but just before their scheduled wedding day he fell through the ice while skating on the Schuylkill River and was lost. Caroline was later known as the "Enchantress of Philadelphia" because of her role as patron of the arts and her wide circle of friends, including painter Cecilia Beaux (1855–1942) and arts philanthropist Isabella Stewart Gardner (1840–1924). This artistic and social colony at Gloucester was nicknamed Dabsville for Joanna Stewart Davidge (c. 1860–1931), A. Piatt Andrew (1873–1936), Cecilia Beaux, and Caroline Sinkler. Some accounts claim that the S in Dabsville was for Henry "Harry" Sleeper (1878–1934). Sleeper, Sinkler, and Andrew lived in a row: "McCann," "Wrong Roof," and "Red Roof." The men in Caroline's circle were much younger than the women.[24]

23. Elizabeth Sinkler Richardson, "Recollections," a four-page, undated typewritten document in the possession of author LeClercq.
24. The wonderful story of summering in Gloucester is told by Joseph E. Garland. The guest book for "Wrong Roof," Carrie's home, is filled with pictures and good tidings from Lizzie, Eck, and all the Southern Sinkler family (Joseph E. Garland, *Eastern Point* [Dublin, N.H.: William L. Bauhan, 1971]). The guest book is owned by Sidney Lockwood Tynan.

Sinkler, Charles (January 8, 1818–March 27, 1894). Charles, Lizzie's father, was the son of William Sinkler (1787–1853) and Elizabeth Allen Broun (1784–1824), who had built Eutaw Plantation in 1808. Charles grew up at Eutaw Plantation and attended the College of Charleston, graduating in 1835. He delivered a public oration entitled "On Eloquence" at a special exhibition of the college on April 4, 1834. He served in the United States Navy as a midshipman, beginning March 24, 1836. He passed midshipman on July 1, 1842. He served in the Gulf of Mexico during the Mexican War as the acting master aboard the U.S. Brig *Perry*. After Vera Cruz his squadron was on the lookout for privateers between Havana and the Florida Keys. On October 11, 1846, the brig *Perry* was wrecked on one of the Florida Keys in a hurricane that destroyed the Keys. He resigned on February 20, 1847. He returned to South Carolina, and he and Emily moved to Belvidere Plantation in 1848, where he commenced cotton farming. Mr. Sinkler did not fight in the Civil War. He was a Unionist, subscribing to such Southern Union newspapers as the *Southern Patriot,* published by Benjamin F. Perry of Greenville, South Carolina. In 1863, when President Lincoln issued the Emancipation Proclamation,[25] he called up the slaves of the plantation and told them they had been proclaimed free by Lincoln, but they had better stay quietly in their comfortable homes. He also told them he intended to divide among them most of his provisions, which he did. On April 11, 1887, he applied for a Mexican War pension.

25. The Emancipation Proclamation was issued by President Abraham Lincoln on September 22, 1862, in an effort to pressure the seceded states into returning to the union. When the document did not have its intended effect, it was enacted into law on January 1, 1863, and freed the slaves. It reads, in part: "That on the first day of January, in the year of our Lord one thousand eight hundred and sixty-three, all persons held as slaves within any State or designated part of a State, the people whereof shall then be in rebellion against the United States, shall be then, thenceforward, and forever free; and the Executive Government of the United States, including the military and naval authority thereof, will recognize and maintain the freedom of such persons, and will do no act or acts to repress such persons, or any of them, in any efforts they may make for their actual freedom. ... And I hereby enjoin upon the people so declared to be free to abstain from all violence, unless in necessary self-defense; and I recommend to them that, in all cases when allowed, they labor faithfully for reasonable wages" (Abraham Lincoln. *Emancipation Proclamation,* http://www.nps.gov/ncro/anti/emancipation.html).

He had previously applied for bounty lands in November 1857 pursuant to an Act of Congress of 1855 awarding bounty land for service in the Mexican War. On March 16, 1854, Charles's brother James Sinkler died and left Charles as the ward of his four children. The correspondence relating to this wardship is contained in the Sinkler Papers in the South Carolina Historical Society.

Sinkler, Charles St. George (October 20, 1853–July 2, 1934). Born at Eutaw Springs in 1853, Charles was the second son of Charles Sinkler (1818–1894) and Emily Wharton (1823–1875), and Lizzie's youngest brother. He graduated from the College of Charleston in 1874. He was involved in politics as a Democratic county chairman from 1883 to 1884. He married Anne Wickham Porcher[26] of St. Juliens Plantation on December 5, 1883. He was the organizer and commander of the Eutaw Light Dragoons, a cavalry company of the state. He and Anne lived at Belvidere until their deaths. He was this author's great-grandfather. His daughters Anne and Emily traveled with Lizzie Sinkler Coxe on many of her memorable expeditions.

Sinkler, Emily Wharton (October 12, 1823–February 10, 1875). Lizzie's mother, Emily Wharton was the third child of Arabella Griffith and Thomas Isaac Wharton. She was born in Philadelphia and lived her younger years at 150 Walnut Street, directly across from the statehouse and Independence Square. Thomas Isaac Wharton was the center of a literary circle as well as a legal circle of distinguished friends. He was a founder of the Pennsylvania Historical Society and was a member of the board of the American Philosophical Society. Emily flourished in this intellectually rich environment. She learned French and Italian in school and became an accomplished pianist and vocalist. She spent her summers with her grandmother, Mary Corré Griffith,[27] at Charlie's Hope on the Delaware River.

---

26. Anne Wickham Porcher (1860–1919) was the daughter of Dr. Julius T. Porcher (1829–1863) and Mary Fanning Wickham (1831–1875).

27. Mary Corré married John Griffith, a merchant in Philadelphia. The Corrés were a French refugee family. Mrs. Griffith was early left a widow with large means and bought land on the Delaware River near Bordentown, which she named Charlie's Hope, after Charles Edward Stuart, the British prince who was nicknamed Bonnie Prince Charlie. The garden at Charlie's Hope was renowned (Anne Sinkler Whaley LeClercq, *Between North and South: The Letters of Emily Wharton Sinkler, 1842–1865* [Columbia: University of South Carolina Press, 2001], 202). Mary

She met and fell in love with Charles Sinkler when he was stationed as a navy midshipman in Philadelphia. They were married on October 8, 1842, in St. Stephen's Episcopal Church in Philadelphia.[28] By November 1842 they had arrived in Charleston and were staying in Stewarts, a boarding-house on Chalmers Street. That fall Emily and Charles moved to Charles's father's home, Eutaw Plantation. Charles remained in the navy until 1847. He resigned after the Mexican War, and the couple moved to Belvidere, an old, decayed plantation built around 1785 by Charles's grandmother, Margaret Cantey Sinkler.[29] At Belvidere, Emily and Charles renovated the many buildings, adding a church for the slaves. Emily's garden was renowned for its beautiful roses and irises. Belvidere bordered the Santee River and Swamp and was consequently very unhealthy in the summer months. Emily and Charles built a home and farm in the Sand Hills[30] at Bradford Springs and called it Woodford. Charles raised cotton at both Belvidere and Woodford. During the 1850s Belvidere and Eutaw plantations became the center of a vigorous intellectual and cultural life for the surrounding

---

Griffith (1779–1846) was a well-known author of books about horticulture and farming, including *Our Neighbourhood, or Letters on Horticulture and Natural Phenomena: Interspersed with Opinions on Domestic and Moral Economy* (New York, 1831).

28. Charles Sinkler entered the U.S. Navy as an acting midshipman in March of 1836. He had a distinguished career with the following highlights: He joined the USS *Columbia* in October of 1837 and sailed under the command of George C. Read on a three-year cruise to the East Indies via the Cape of Good Hope and visited China in 1839, returning finally to Boston on June 13 on March 1840. He was addressed to Philadelphia in October 1840 and attended the naval school there in 1841. He passed midshipman on July 1, 1842. He was furloughed for eight months in 1842, during which time he married Emily Wharton Sinkler, and then in November of 1843 he served as acting master of the USS *Consort* in the African Squadron. In 1844 he was made acting master of the Charleston Naval Station. In 1846 he was made acting master of the USS *Perry* and sailed for the West Indies under the command of George S. Blake. The ship was thrown on a reef off the Florida coast during a hurricane on October 12, 1846. On February 20, 1847, his resignation from the navy was accepted (U.S. Navy record of Charles Sinkler, in possession of author LeClercq).

29. Margaret Cantey (1763–1821) was the third wife of Capt. James Sinkler (1740–1800) of Old Santee and the daughter of Ann Drake and Charles Cantey.

30. Bradford Springs is near Sumter, South Carolina.

French Huguenot community.[31] Emily and Charles had six children: Elizabeth Allen Sinkler (Lizzie), born July 7, 1843; Wharton Sinkler (Bud), born August 7, 1845; Arabella Wharton Sinkler, born November 24, 1847; Charles St. George Sinkler (Charlie), born October 20, 1853; Mary Wharton Sinkler, born March 25, 1857; and Caroline Sidney Sinkler (Carrie), born April 23, 1860. Emily and Charles remained at Belvidere during the Civil War. They resumed cotton farming in 1866. Emily died tragically on the way home from an Ash Wednesday service on February 10, 1875.[32]

Sinkler, Wharton (August 7, 1845–March 16, 1910). Wharton was Emily and Charles's second child and first son and was Lizzie's brother. He was affectionately called Bud by his sister Lizzie. He fought in the Civil War at the age of seventeen on the side of the Confederacy, and was stationed in North Carolina. His loyal slave, Mingo Rivers,[33] accompanied him to battle and came home periodically to get new provisions for them both. Wharton wrote many letters home to his mother, Emily, during the war, and they are located in the South Carolina Historical Society in the Sinkler

31. The French Huguenot community settled along the Santee River in the 1690s. They built a distinctive style of plantation house of unpainted cypress. They were cotton planters with large tracts of land and numerous slaves. Their lifestyle revolved around farming, horse racing, and visits to Charleston.

32. Emily Wharton Sinkler's headstone at Rocks Church cemetery near Eutawville, S.C., reads: "Daughter of Isaac P. Wharton of Philadelphia, Pa. and wife of Charles Sinkler of this parish / killed on Ash Wednesday by a run-away horse" (*The Rocks Church Cemetery Burial List*, http://www.rootsweb.com/~scbchs/cemlist.htm [accessed March 26, 2004]).

33. "The body servants of the Confederate soldiers were more intimately associated with their masters than any of the others. In many cases, soldiers and servants had been childhood playmates. Each had a genuine affection for the other, which was cemented by common exposure and hardship in the army" (Bell Irvin Wiley, *Southern Negroes, 1861–1865* [Baton Rouge: Louisiana State University Press, 1938, 1974], 64). Ford stated that as many as twenty-five soldiers in a particular South Carolina company were accompanied by servants. "As a rule, only commissioned officers retained servants after the first year of the war" (Arthur Peronneau Ford, *Life in the Confederate Army: Being Personal Experiences of a Private Soldier in the Confederate Army, with Some Experiences and Sketches of Southern Life, by Marion Johnstone Ford* [New York and Washington, D.C.: Neale Publishing, 1905], 11; also referenced in Bell Irwin Wiley, *Southern Negroes 1861–1865* [Baton Rouge: Louisiana State University Press, 1938], 134).

papers. Wharton left the South after the war and studied medicine at the University of Pennsylvania. He returned South every year for long hunting parties at Belvidere. He became a famous neurologist in Philadelphia. Wharton was married to Ella Brock on February 10, 1872, and their children included Julia Ursula Sinkler (b. 1872); Wharton Sinkler Jr. (1885–1967), who married Louise Broomell Elkins;[34] Francis Wharton Sinkler (b. 1877); Charles Sinkler (b. 1874); Seaman Deas Sinkler (1879–1927). who married Emilie Beauveau Rhodes (1882–1955); John Penn Brock Sinkler (1875–1959); Emily Wharton Sinkler (1881–1884); and Ella "Elsie" Brock Sinkler (b. 1887).

Sinkler, William (November 2, 1787–June 8, 1853). Lizzie's grandfather was a central figure in her life, growing up at Eutaw and Belvidere Plantations. William Sinkler (the *beau-père*)[35] was the oldest son of Capt. James Sinkler (1740–1800) and his third wife, Margaret Cantey (1763–1821). He was Lizzie's grandfather. He built Eutaw Plantation in 1808 and married Elizabeth Allen Broun (1784–1824) on January 16, 1810. Their children were James Sinkler (1810–1854), who married Margaret Huger (1813–1888); Seaman Deas Sinkler (1816–1847); Charles Sinkler (1818–1894), who married Emily Wharton (1823–1875) of Philadelphia; Elizabeth Allen Sinkler (1821–1908), who married Col. Richard Irvine Manning II (1817–1861); and William Henry Sinkler (1819–1856), who married his first cousin Anna Linton Thomson (1823–1873). The *beau-père* had immense landholdings in Upper St. John's, much of it prime cotton land and the remainder pinelands. When William Sinkler died in 1853, he left 103 slaves to his three sons. He left James Sinkler two tracts of land, Brackey and Brushpond. He left the Belvidere estate and four hundred acres of swampland adjoining it to Charles Sinkler. He left Eutaw Plantation to William Henry Sinkler. To Charles and William Henry, he left the plantation called

---

34. According to Louise Broomell Elkins Sinkler (1890–1977), "Our wedding was to have been a large and gay affair, but the death of Wharton's father prevented that" (Louise Sinkler, *Leaves Folded Down* [Wayne, Pa.: Haverford House, 1971], 29).

35. The term *beau-père* is French for "fair father" and was intended to signify endearment.

Dorcher.[36] He is buried in St. Stephen's Episcopal Church[37] in St. Stephen's, South Carolina. On his grave is the following: "In memory of William Sinkler, esq. who was born on the 2nd of Nov. 1787 and died June 1853 aged 65 years. The Angel of the Lord encampeth round about them that fear him and delivereth them." He was Lizzie's grandfather and lived at Eutaw Plantation, which he had built in 1808.

Sinkler, William Henry (1819–1856). The youngest brother of Charles Sinkler, William Henry died when only thirty-seven years old. He is buried at the Rocks Church, and his headstone reads, "Blessed are the pure of heart, they shall see God." He was married to his first cousin Anna Linton Thomson, who had been the ward of William Sinkler, the *beau-père*. They lived at Eutaw Plantation, which they inherited from William Sinkler.

Wharton, Arabella Griffith (1800–February 27, 1866). Arabella Griffith was Emily's mother. After marrying Thomas Isaac Wharton (1791–1857)· she was never in good health and seemed especially to have eye problems. Lizzie often stayed with her in Philadelphia.

Wharton, Francis (March 7, 1820–February 21, 1889). Emily Wharton Sinkler's older brother Frank graduated from Yale University in 1839 and went on to become a clergyman, educator, and author.[38] On November 4, 1852, he married Sydney Paul, daughter of Comegys Paul and Sarah Rodman. Sydney Paul Wharton died in September 1854, and Frank then married Helen Elizabeth Ashhurst on December 27, 1860. Two children were born from this marriage: Mary Ashhurst Wharton, born November 13, 1861, and Ella Wharton, born May 29, 1863.

Wharton, Henry (June 2, 1827–November 11, 1880). Henry Wharton was Lizzie's Philadelphia uncle. He worked as a lawyer with his father, Thomas

---

36. "Will of William Sinkler," *Record of Wills, Charleston County, South Carolina,* vol. 46A (1851–56), 292–96, available at the Charleston County Library.

37. St. Stephen's Parish Church, built circa 1764, is a National Historic Landmark (William P. Baldwin, *Plantations of the Low Country South Carolina 1697–1865* [Greensboro: Legacy Publications, 1985], 89).

38. Some of Francis Wharton's works include *Wharton's Criminal Law, Wharton's Criminal Procedure, Wharton's Criminal Evidence,* and other works related to jurisprudence.

Isaac Wharton (1791–1857) and later as a Philadelphia prosecutor. Henry graduated from the University of Pennsylvania in 1846 with a Bachelor of Arts degree, and in 1849 with a Master of Arts degree. He married Katharine Johnstone Brinley[39] on October 21, 1858, and they had six children. Lizzie was very fond of her Uncle Henry and Aunt Kate. A portrait of Henry Wharton is located in the Library Company of Philadelphia. Entries in the Library Company minutes[40] indicate that the picture was commissioned and purchased as a memorial to Wharton, who had been a board member of the Library Company for eighteen years.

Wharton, Thomas Isaac (May 17, 1791–April 7, 1857). Lizzie's devoted grandfather, known affectionately as "Party," was a Philadelphia lawyer and a distinguished jurist with a specialty in property law. He was the son of Isaac Wharton (1745–1808) and Margaret Rawle. After graduating from the University of Pennsylvania in 1807, Thomas Isaac began the study of law in the office of his uncle William Rawle (1759–1836), a leader of the Philadelphia bar. Though Thomas Isaac was especially learned in real-property law, his knowledge in other legal fields was hardly less profound. Among his early labors was that of compiling a *Digest of Cases Adjudged in the Circuit Court of the United States for the Third Circuit, and in the Courts of Pennsylvania* (1822). In 1830 he was appointed with William Rawle and Joel Jones to codify the civil statute law of Pennsylvania, a task that consumed four years. There is extensive Wharton material in the manuscript section of the Pennsylvania Historical Society.

39. Henry Wharton's wife, Kate, kept a diary during the Civil War detailing her "daily routine, which incorporated chores, visitors, and her family, both in Philadelphia and Newport, Rhode Island" (Diaries Collection no. 1861, Historical Society of Pennsylvania, http://www.hsp.org/ [accessed July 20, 2005]). Please note: the Historical Society of Pennsylvania misspells Katharine Johnstone Brinley Wharton's name as Katherine Johnson Brinley Wharton or Katherine Johnston Brinley Wharton. In 1901 Kate Wharton (1834–1925) wrote a twenty-three–page genealogical memoir of her grandfather Edward Brinley (1757–1851), entitled "An Old Newport Loyalist." This work was later published in a 1920 issue of *Bulletin of the Newport Historical Society.*

40. The Library Company was founded by Benjamin Franklin in 1731 as one of the first subscription libraries in colonial America (*A Brief History of the Library Company of Philadelphia,* http://www.librarycompany.org/instance.htm [accessed March 26, 2004]).

Descendents of Tench Coxe

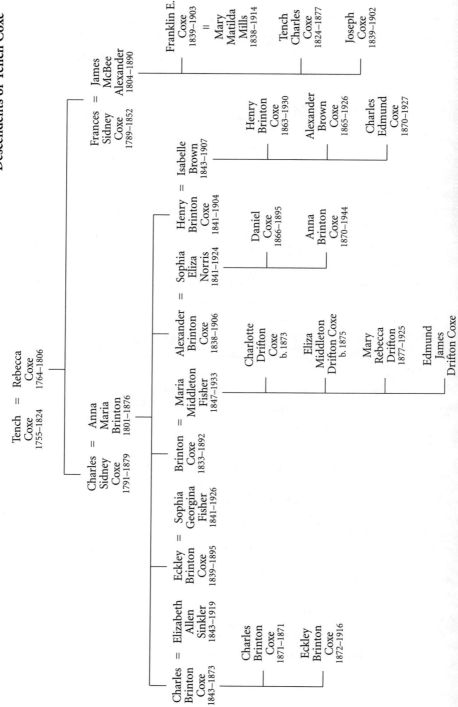

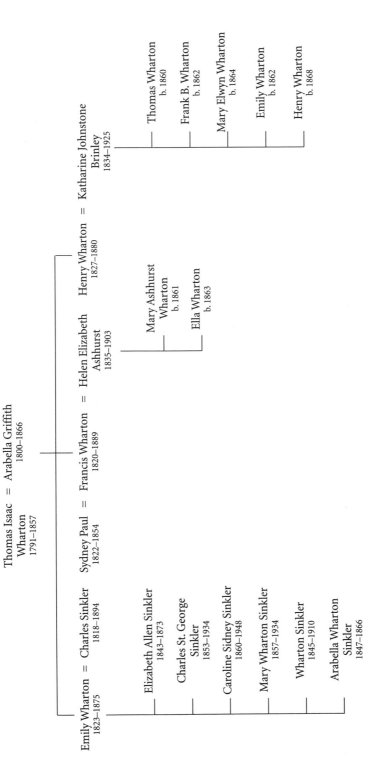

Thomas Isaac = Arabella Griffith
Wharton   1800–1866
1791–1857

Emily Wharton = Charles Sinkler   Sydney Paul = Francis Wharton = Helen Elizabeth   Henry Wharton = Katharine Johnstone
1823–1875   1818–1894   1822–1854   1820–1889   Ashhurst   1827–1880   Brinley
                                                                   1835–1903   1834–1925

Elizabeth Allen Sinkler
1843–1873

Charles St. George
Sinkler
1853–1934

Caroline Sidney Sinkler
1860–1948

Mary Wharton Sinkler
1857–1934

Wharton Sinkler
1845–1910

Arabella Wharton
Sinkler
1847–1866

Mary Ashhurst
Wharton
b. 1861

Ella Wharton
b. 1863

Thomas Wharton
b. 1860

Frank B. Wharton
b. 1862

Mary Elwyn Wharton
b. 1864

Emily Wharton
b. 1862

Henry Wharton
b. 1868

Elizabeth Sinkler Coxe's
Tales from the Grand Tour
1890–1910

CHAPTER ONE

⚜

Living between North and South

Elizabeth Allen Sinkler Coxe (July 7, 1843–October 24, 1919), known affectionately as Lizzie and later as Auntie to her nieces, was the eldest of six children born to Emily Wharton and Charles Sinkler. The Sinkler family lived at Eutaw and Belvidere plantations in Eutawville, South Carolina. They spent each summer in Philadelphia with their grandparents, Thomas Isaac Wharton (1791–1857) and Arabella Griffith Wharton (1800–1866). Lizzie grew up living between North and South, with innumerable friends and family in each region.

Lizzie was the oldest of five children. Wharton Sinkler (1845–1910) was Lizzie's beloved brother and companion. Wharton left home to fight for the Confederacy at the age of seventeen. Next was Charles St. George Sinkler (1853–1934). Charlie, as he was affectionately known, was a great horseman, hunter, and Southern gentleman, and married Anne Wickham Porcher (1860–1919). Anne and Charlie had three daughters, Emily, Anne, and Caroline. Next was Mary Wharton Sinkler (1857–1934), who married Charles Stevens (1854–1928) and had two daughters, Elizabeth and Laura. Seventeen years separated Lizzie and Caroline Sidney Sinkler (Carrie), the youngest daughter, born on April 23, 1860. Lizzie and her youngest sister were inseparable companions, living and traveling together. The Sinklers lived at Belvidere Plantation during the winter months of the year, at their Sumter County farm, Woodford, during the late spring and summer, and spent the late summer and early fall in Philadelphia. They vacationed in Flat Rock, North Carolina, or Sullivan's Island, near Charleston, South Carolina.

Lizzie grew up at Eutaw and Belvidere, the Sinklers' cotton plantations in Upper St. John's Parish, South Carolina. The plantations bordered the

Santee River, which was rich with game and old-growth cypress trees. It had once been the home of the Eutaw Indians.[1] During the American Revolution, Francis Marion[2] and his band conducted guerrilla warfare from the Santee River to the Pee Dee River. Built in 1795 of cypress, the Belvidere house was Lizzie's Southern home. It was built fourteen feet up on a brick basement and was entered via a long flight of brick stairs. A garden, redolent with sweet olive trees, perfumed the air on either side of the scrolling banisters. The house was entered through double doors, one door into the sitting room and the other into the dining room.

This was the center of Lizzie's young life. The family gathered each morning in the sitting parlor for prayers. A hearty breakfast was served in the dining room with waffles, hot corn cakes, hominy, wheat toast, ham, duck sausage, eggs, and milk, tea, and coffee. After breakfast Emily taught Lizzie to sing and play the piano; Lizzie became a skilled musician. Emily also taught Lizzie to read and write at the young age of two. Lizzie learned to keep a diary and wrote weekly letters to her grandparents in Philadelphia. Lizzie and her brother Wharton (called Bud) were taught by Irish tutors. She was an avid reader of the nineteenth-century literary greats, including Tennyson and Wordsworth, committing many of their poems to heart. Emily taught Lizzie fluent French as well as Italian. During the morning the ladies of the house sat on the porch sewing while one of them read aloud. Lizzie sat close to the group, absorbing the excitement of Charles Dickens's *Dombey and Sons* or the pathos of Charlotte Brontë's *Jane Eyre*. The newspapers of both Charleston and Philadelphia serialized contemporary novels as they appeared.

---

1. The Eutaw Indians belonged to a tribe of South Carolina coastal Indians called the Cusabo. The Cusabo tribes included the Ashepoo, Combahee, Edisto, Kiawah, Stono, Wando, and others. (Chapman J. Milling, *Red Carolinians* [Columbia: University of South Carolina Press, 1969], 35). The Cusabo spoke Muskhogean, a family of languages shared by peoples living in what is now the southeastern United States. The name *Cusabo* may be derived from the Catawba Indian term for "Coosawhatchie River (people)" (John R. Swanton, *The Indian Tribes of North America* [Washington, D.C.: U.S. Government Printing Office, 1953], 94–96). The word *Eutaw* is thought to mean pine tree in the Cherokee language.

2. Revolutionary War hero Francis Marion (1732–1795) was a distant relative of Lizzie Sinkler's family through the Cordes relatives, part of the Huguenot community that settled near the Santee River.

While life at Belvidere followed the daily routines of a farming community, visits to Charleston for the February races were filled with excitement. Lizzie was part of the family entourage staying with her grandfather, the *beau-père,* William Sinkler, at his suite in the Charleston Hotel. Built by Charles F. Reichardt,[3] the Charleston Hotel was grand, with thirteen granite Corinthian columns fronting Meeting Street. The elegant public rooms of the hotel were furnished in the latest cut velvets from Genoa and featured rosewood and mahogany furniture from New York and Philadelphia.

The races always took place during the third week of February at the Washington Race Course. There was a classical designed ladies' pavilion, where Lizzie and her family viewed the *beau-père's* winning horses. Year after year, whether it was Jeff Davis, or Shark, or Jeannette Berkeley, the red and white silks of Eutaw Plantation won the money prizes. The *beau-père* had a racetrack at his plantation, Eutaw, and there his trainer, Hercules, a slave with a rare talent for horse training, trained one winner after another. Lizzie thrilled to the excitement of the one-mile heat, enjoying a crowd that brought country aristocracy together with Charleston blue bloods.[4]

3. Charles F. Reichardt, a Prussian architect, also designed the ladies' pavilion at the racetrack on the grounds of the present-day Hampton Park in Charleston, S.C. He was said to be a pupil of Karl Friedrich Schinkel, a German proponent of the Greek Revival style (Jane. E. Allen, "Horse Racing Was Once a Popular Pastime in Charleston," *News and Courier,* March 14, 1983).

4. The races began on Wednesday and lasted through Saturday. The Jockey Club purse of one thousand dollars was for four one-mile heats, a grueling race. In the 1848 race William Sinkler entered Shark. Before an animated crowd and on a blustery cold day, Shark carried the field against Countess and Bostona. The Jockey Club Ball was held on Friday night. "The company consisted of much of the beauty and fashion of our city. . . . The supper was elegant indeed. The centers of the tables were set off by pyramids of confectionary and classically formed temples, glittering with pendant bonbons" ("Our Race," *Charleston Courier,* February 19 and 22–24, 1848). Lizzie's Uncle Henry Wharton was also at this race and described it with gusto: "The races occupied nearly the whole of the day time of the week, and they were to me extremely fascinating from, not only the beauty of the sight, but the part which Mr. Sinkler took in them. His horse 'Shark' a most magnificent animal won two purses. . . . But my time was occupied still more agreeably in the evenings. Tuesday evening I went to the St. Cecilia Ball. . . . There I was introduced to a number of young ladies. . . . Wednesday was the dinner of the Race Club, a very splendid affair. Real turtle soup, wild turkies, venison, grouse,

There were wonderful festivities each year for Christmas. No one stayed in Charleston for the Christmas season. All of the Sinklers gathered at Eutaw Plantation, where there was an enormous fir tree emblazoned with wax candles. The *beau-père* turned his front piazza over to the slaves for three afternoons during Christmas. There was dancing, music from bones, drums, and the fiddle of Orlando, a talented slave musician. Lizzie and her black playmates were in the thick of the festivities.

Emily, Charles, and the children paid yearly summer visits to Philadelphia to stay with Thomas Isaac Wharton and Arabella Griffith Wharton. This was Lizzie's Northern home. Lizzie adored her "Party," as she called grandfather Thomas Isaac Wharton. Together they explored the fairs in Germantown and took the cars to Fairmont Park. Lizzie exchanged letters with Party[5] and with Marty, as grandmother Arabella Griffith Wharton was called, and also had a running correspondence with her uncles Frank and Henry Wharton.

The Wharton house in Philadelphia at 150 Walnut Street was brick with a white marble stairway to the first floor. Thomas Isaac Wharton's friends were the influential men of letters and the successful lawyers of his day. He had founded the Pennsylvania Historical Society, and there were frequent gatherings of illustrious men and women at his home. It was in Philadelphia that Lizzie made friends with the Cadwaladers, Coxes, and other prominent Philadelphia young people.

Emily and her daughter Lizzie were like twins, inseparable and much alike. They read German and French together in the long afternoons at Belvidere. They entertained evening guests with piano duets or with Emily singing the songs of Jenny Lind or the arias of Rossini. They supervised the kitchen help as Lizzie learned to make her mother's favorite charlotte russe

---

partridges, pheasants, shad, and all the smaller fry of delicacies, not forgetting pate de foie gras in great abundance, and wines of great value, such as Johannisberg of 1822" (Henry Wharton to Frank Wharton, March 1, 1848, letter in the possession of author LeClercq).

5. In a letter dated December 15, 1851, and addressed to Lizzie and her brother "Buddy," grandfather Thomas Isaac "Party" Wharton writes, "I am sorry that we can't send any Christmas presents just now because the steamers are stopped, but I hope to find some way yet" (Sinkler Family Papers 1802–51, South Carolina Historical Society, Charleston, South Carolina).

desserts and trifles for dinner parties.[6] They shopped together for cloth in Charleston at Mrs. Hanney's at 375 King Street. They purchased the latest in cut velvets from Italy, mantillas from Paris, and silk flowers from Naples. They shared a love for the same wonderful blue silk dresses with exquisite hand-sewn lace collars and cuffs. Lizzie learned style, grace, and wisdom at her mother's knee.

Lizzie grew up in an antebellum world that included the pageantry of chivalry and the struggles of slavery. The Sinkler lives centered on the French Huguenot community of Eutawville and the twenty-five or so plantations that rimmed the Santee River. Lizzie knew the gospel songs of the slaves. She knew the planting cycle of a cotton plantation by heart: fall preparation of the fields, winter baling of cotton, spring cultivation of the tiny new plants, and summer's long growth and maturation of the cotton bolls. Belvidere with its slave "street" was a constant hum of black African activity. Lizzie grew up in the midst of a slave-dependent society, understanding its nuances, its customs, and its mutual dependencies. This was in sharp contrast to urban life in the 1850s in Philadelphia.

Like her mother, Emily, Lizzie loved to write. All during her life she kept detailed journals of her daily adventures. She was also a prolific correspondent. Lizzie was seventeen at the onset of the Civil War. She described that experience in her *Memories of a South Carolina Plantation during the War,* which she published in 1912 from a diary kept during the war. Lizzie's *Memories* covered the entire five years of the war with its privations and terrors. Belvidere was twenty-five miles from the railroad and sixty miles from Charleston. It saw no active involvement until the last winter and spring of the war. Sherman's troops marched through Bamberg, South Carolina, twenty-five miles to the northwest.

As the war wore on, the family at Belvidere became increasingly isolated. Lizzie wrote, "there was a terrible dearth of news after this (Sherman's

---

6. Emily's receipt for trifle was as follows: "Fill the bottom of a large dish with cake broken into small pieces and moisten with a little wine. Put 1 quart of cream into a deep bowl and sweeten to taste with very fine sugar. Beat the whites of 2 eggs very stiff in another vessel and add to the cream. Then churn to stiff froth which as it rises, skim off and put on cake. It must be beaten in a cool place" (Anne Sinkler Whaley LeClercq, *An Antebellum Plantation Household: Including the South Carolina Low Country Receipts and Remedies of Emily Wharton Sinkler* [Columbia, S.C.: University of South Carolina Press, 1996], 99).

burning of Columbia), and we scarcely ever received a letter; and newspapers, of course, no longer existed. At this time when people were afraid to leave home, and we had no guests staying with us, my mother and I read through many volumes of French and English history, and she taught me German so successfully that we read with ease and pleasure most of Schiller's and Goethe's works."[7]

The end of slavery produced economic uncertainty for the Sinkler family and for the future of farming at Belvidere. Lizzie described her father's actions on hearing of the Emancipation Proclamation: "My father called up the plantation and told them they had been proclaimed free by Lincoln, but they had better stay quietly in their comfortable homes. He also told them he intended to divide among them most of his provisions, which he did. This, of course, was considered quite quixotic by his neighbours."[8]

Because Charles had served in the United States Navy, he knew several Union colleagues stationed at the Charleston harbor. Lizzie described the arrival of a gunboat sent up the Santee by Admiral Dahlgren to deliver a letter to Charles. The emissary was invited into the house, and "papa said he was very glad to hear from his old friend and classmate, Dahlgren, but on reading his letter he said very stiffly to O'Kane: 'I am surprised to see that Dahlgren writes he supposes I am loyal to the United States. He knows very well that my loyalty belongs first to my State and only through my State to the government.'"[9]

Belvidere was attacked by Union soldiers that included a Negro brigade. Lizzie described the scene and her family's reaction:

> At last on this lovely spring day, after hours of anxiety, we looked out from the piazza and saw a number of negro soldiers running into the yard. Of course, the sight of negroes in uniform seemed to us an appalling thing, for nowadays it is difficult to imagine what a crime and horrible menace the arming the negroes appeared to the South. Our own coloured servants came to the piazza and stood by us. The soldiers whooped and yelled for all the plantation to gather. They broke open the storerooms, smokehouse, and barns, and threw out to the negroes all the provisions and things they

7. Elizabeth A. Coxe, *Memories of a South Carolina Plantation during the War* (Philadelphia: Privately printed, 1912), 35.
8. Ibid., 36.
9. Ibid., 39.

could find. At last several of them ran up the back steps and without even looking at us where we stood on the piazza went into the house and began throwing things about cursing and swearing, lashing long carriage whips about our heads and saying "Dammed rebels" very often. Maumer (a loyal house servant) went with my mother after them into the house and tried to stop their injuring things, continually reproaching them for their misconduct. One of the Negro soldiers snatched at my mother's watch chain and she took it off and put it into his hands. He looked at the locket hanging on the chain and said: "Do you value the hair in this locket?" Yes, said she. He took his knife and picked the hair out and gave it to her. His conscience then seemed to stab him, and I am sure her beauty and lovely expression moved him, for he threw the whole thing, watch and chain, back into her hands and ran away as if from temptation.[10]

The Civil War was a time of distress for the Sinklers, not only because of the privations of the war but also because of the fear and anxiety they had for Wharton, who had enlisted in the Confederate Army at the age of sixteen. Emily Sinkler expressed her concern for her son Wharton in a letter to her brother Henry Wharton in Philadelphia: "We have not heard from our dear boy since that letter of March 3, but a person who is a paroled prisoner told an intelligent servant of ours that he was captured two weeks ago at the same time he was, and he was unhurt, that he saw him after he was taken. This all seems straight but we must not give it much creed. But oh dear Hen this state of uncertainty we are in about him, the not being able to hear and yet knowing the constant danger he is in is most harrowing to my soul. Pray for him and for me."[11]

When the war was finally over, the Sinklers were among the first to leave South Carolina, returning for a year to Philadelphia. Belvidere and its freed slaves were left under the supervision of a caretaker from Ohio. However, friends and neighbors begged Charles Sinkler to come back to South Carolina, and the whole family returned and resumed life at Belvidere again in 1867. Lizzie described it as a time of the greatest privation, when staples such as coffee and sugar were unavailable and old clothes were recycled to make do.

10. Ibid., 44–45.
11. Emily Wharton Sinkler to Henry Wharton, April 4, 1865, Sinkler Family Papers, South Carolina Historical Society, Charleston, South Carolina.

While Lizzie was living at Belvidere during the Civil War, her husband-to-be, Charles Brinton Coxe, was in the Union Cavalry. Charles had graduated from the University of Pennsylvania in 1862 and from there went immediately into the Union Cavalry. He was from a distinguished Philadelphia family, one on friendly terms with the Whartons. Charles served in Rush's Lancers[12] as an officer. The account of his life during the period 1863–65 is contained in a series of letters to his best and dearest friend, John Cadwalader (1843–1925).[13] The two graduated from the University of Pennsylvania together, had been in the same fraternity, Delta Phi,[14] and had a long friendship from youth. Charles was only twenty years old during the war, and his letters reveal a lonely young man trying to cope with the tedium of camp life. He missed the parties and friendships of Philadelphia and yearned to hear home gossip. Charles and Lizzie had vastly different Civil War experiences. Their union bridged a gulf that divided the nation. Lizzie had many Low Country beaux; however, her parents disapproved of all, hoping instead for a Philadelphia match. Finally, when Lizzie was twenty-seven she married Charles Brinton Coxe of Pennsylvania. The Whartons, Coxes, Cadwaladers, Wilcoxes, and Fishers were warm friends all living near one another in Philadelphia.

Charles Brinton Coxe was the fifth son of Judge Charles Sidney Coxe.[15] He was born in Philadelphia on February 4, 1843, and received a degree from the University of Pennsylvania in 1862. He served in the Union army during the Civil War, first as a lieutenant, then as a captain, and finally as

12. Charles Brinton Coxe (1843–1873) served in the 6th Pennsylvania Cavalry (also known as the 70th Regiment of Pennsylvania Volunteers), which was commanded by Col. Richard Henry Rush (1825–1893), great-grandson of noted Philadelphia physician Benjamin Rush (1745–1813). Col. Rush armed his regiment with lances, hence the name "Rush's Lancers" (Wittenberg, *The Union Cavalry Comes of Age: Hartwood Church to Brandy Station, 1863* [Washington, D.C.: Brassey's, 2003], 100, 137).

13. This series of letters, dated from December 2, 1862, through February 16, 1865, can be found at the Pennsylvania Historical Society in the Cadwalader Collection, John Cadwalader Jr. Section (hereafter referred to as Cadwalader-JCJS).

14. The Delta Phi fraternity is considered the oldest American fraternity, founded in 1827 at Union College.

15. Charles Sidney Coxe (1791–1879) was a son of Tench Coxe (1755–1824) and Rebecca Coxe (1764–1806), who may have been related to each other.

a major of the 6th Pennsylvania Cavalry, which was known at the outbreak of the war as Rush's Lancers. He became a member of Coxe Brothers & Company, which became the largest coal producers in post–Civil War America. On June 1, 1870, Lizzie and Charles were married. Mr. Coxe and his brother Eckley Brinton Coxe (1839–1895) were early developers of anthracite coal mines. Other siblings included Alexander "Aleck" Brinton Coxe (1838–1906),[16] Brinton Coxe (1833–1892), Henry Brinton Coxe (1841–1904),[17] and several other brothers and sisters, some of whom did not reach adulthood.

With the war over Charles and his brother Eckley, who was also a well-schooled and capable mining engineer, returned to family property in Drifton, Pennsylvania. Eckley had spent the years from 1860 through 1864 in Europe studying a number of subjects including engineering, accounting, languages, art, and mining. Tench Coxe,[18] the boys' grandfather, had acquired large tracts of relatively untillable land in the anthracite[19] regions

16. Alexander "Aleck" Brinton Coxe (1838–1906) was graduated from the University of Pennsylvania in 1856, served as an aide to Maj. Gen. George Gordon Meade (1815–1872) during the Civil War, and helped establish Coxe Brothers and Company with his brothers Charles, Eckley, Henry, and Brinton and cousin Franklin Coxe. Aleck married Sophia Eliza Norris (1841–1924) and lived in Drifton. Later, as the sole surviving brother, Aleck sold the family's mining interests to the Lehigh Valley Railroad Company in 1905.

17. Henry Brinton Coxe (1841–1904) married Isabelle (or Isabella) Brown (1843–1907) on February 13, 1862, and they had three children: Henry Brinton Coxe Jr. (1863–1930), Alexander Brown Coxe (1865–1926), and Charles Edmond Coxe (1870–1927). Henry Jr. and Alexander served as estate agents in 1906, when the last of the original Coxe Brothers partners died.

18. Tench Coxe (1755–1824) was a prominent Philadelphia economist and land speculator, known for his shrewdness in recognizing coal's future importance. Coxe was Pennsylvania's delegate to the Continental Congress and also served as an assistant to Secretary of the Treasury Alexander Hamilton ("Tench Coxe," *Dictionary of American Biography,* Base Set, American Council of Learned Societies, 1928–36; reproduced in *Biography Resource Center* [Farmington Hills: Gale Group, 2004], http://galenet.galegroup.com/servlet/BioRC [accessed June 27, 2005]). President John Adams (1735–1826) described Tench Coxe as "wily, wining, subtle, and insidious."

19. Because of its high carbon content, anthracite coal is a more efficient fuel than bituminous coal as it produces little smoke and more heat and it burns longer and cleaner.

of eight states including northeastern Pennsylvania and western North Carolina long before the importance of coal was realized. Apparently the Coxes knew of its value, as Eckley and Aleck were educated with the intention that they would develop mining operations. Eck was educated to handle the engineering aspects of the enterprise while Aleck dealt with the business side. "At the age of nineteen he [Eckley] was graduated from the University of Pennsylvania. After graduation he continued for a time at the university, studying science, French, and bookkeeping. During his college course his summers had been spent in the coal regions, and in 1859 he assisted in surveying the family's lands. In 1860 he went to Paris where he spent two years at the school of mines, after which he attended for a year the famous mining academy at Freiberg in Saxony. . . . Coxe spent nearly two years more in Europe studying the actual operations of mines in England and on the Continent."[20]

In 1865, Eckley, Charles, Henry, Brinton, and Aleck moved from Philadelphia to Drifton, Pennsylvania, where they set up Coxe Brothers & Company with their cousin Franklin Coxe (1839–1903).[21] On June 27, 1868, Eckley married Sophia G. Fisher,[22] the daughter of Joshua Francis Fisher (1807–1873)[23] of Philadelphia, and Elizabeth Izard Middleton (1815–1890)

20. Eckley Brinton Coxe Sr. (1839–1895) was a renowned mining engineer who invented and improved mining processes and equipment and held more than seventy patents related to mechanical stoking ("Eckley Brinton Coxe," *Dictionary of American Biography,* Base Set, American Council of Learned Societies, 1928–36; reproduced in *Biography Resource Center* [Farmington Hills: Gale Group, 2004], http://galenet.galegroup.com/servlet/BioRC [accessed June 27, 2005]).

21. Franklin E. Coxe (1839–1903) was born in Rutherford, N.C., a son of Francis Sidney Coxe (1789–1852) and Jane McBee Alexander (1804–1890). Frank's father, Francis Sidney Coxe, was a brother of Charles Sidney Coxe (1791–1879).

22. Sophia Georgina Fisher Coxe (1841–1926) was known as the "Angel of the Coalfields" for her charitable and philanthropic acts of kindness and generosity for the coal miners and their families (James J. Bohning, "Angel of the Anthracite: The Philanthropic Legacy of Sophia Georgina Coxe," *Canal History and Technology Proceedings* [2005]: 150–82). N.b.: some sources spell Sophia's middle name as Georgianna and others as Georgina.

23. Joshua Francis Fisher (1807–1873) was described by his granddaughter Sophia Cadwalader (1867–1955) as "a man of rare cultivation and literary taste. . . . Everything prospered till the time of the Civil War. His wife, of course, was intensely Southern in her feelings, he himself took the legal point of view as to the

of Charleston, South Carolina. Brinton married Sophia G. Coxe's sister Maria Middleton Fisher (1847–1933). Aleck married Sophia Eliza Norris (1841–1924) of Baltimore.

Charles settled in Drifton, recovered from the war and worked with Eckley to establish the mining business. In September of 1865 he wrote his friend John Cadwalader,[24] now a well respected lawyer in Philadelphia, that "watering places do not suit my constitution" and that he was "enjoying the quietness of my family."[25] Shortly after this letter Charles wrote Cadwalader that he and his brother Eckley were "setting up a dirty little office" and had been arranging for our "Pic-nic" up here. He believed that it would be a "success," or "at any rate we shall try our best to make it so."[26]

We know from *Memories of a South Carolina Plantation during the War* that Charles Sinkler, along with Emily, Lizzie, and the whole family, returned to Philadelphia and lived there during 1865 and 1866. The Sinklers moved back to Belvidere in 1867. Lizzie had a wide circle of friends in Philadelphia, many of whom wrote to her at Belvidere on a weekly basis. In one letter of January 1867, from Minnie Wilcox, there is mention of Sophie Fisher, Eckley Coxe, and the Fourth Street Cadwaladers. The letter gives a glimpse into Philadelphia life of the time: "The Fishers gave a talking party last week for Miss Jay who has been staying at the 4th St. Cadwaladers, and for whom there has been some attempt at gayety lately. I did not go but heard that it was more successful than the Fishers' parties generally are. Maria is looking very pretty this winter and seems to be much

---

right of Secession; and the way the war was conducted, the indignities offered to Southerners or Southern sympathisers, increased all their feelings ten-fold. On the other hand, the daughters just growing up had very strong sentiments for the young men of their acquaintance going off to join the Northern Army, and so, much family distress ensued" (Sophia H. Cadwalader, ed., *Recollections of Joshua Francis Fisher Written in 1864* [Boston: D. B. Updike, Merrymount Press, 1929], ix, x).

24. According to his obituary, John Cadwalader (1843–1925) was "dean of the Philadelphia Bar, prominent Democrat and member of one of the oldest and most distinguished families in Philadelphia" ("John Cadwalader Dies at 81 Years." *New York Times*, March 13, 1925).

25. Coxe to Cadwalader, Drifton, September 6, 1865, and September 11, 1865, Cadwalader-JCJS.

26. Ibid.

more in the humor for society. Of Sophie I have seen very little and only know that Eckley Coxe is still very devoted to her and that the family manifests a profound ignorance whenever they are asked about her engagement to him."[27]

The Sinklers returned to Belvidere in 1867 and resumed cotton farming. Lizzie described it as the hardest time of her life with nothing but the bare necessities. The Sinklers continued to return to Philadelphia every May for the summer season. Wharton was enrolled at the University of Pennsylvania medical school, another reason for the family to keep in regular touch with Philadelphia.

Because the family was so comfortable living between North and South, it is not surprising that Lizzie Sinkler and Charles Coxe knew each other. Philadelphia society was a relatively tight knit group. Whartons, Cadwaladers, Fishers, Wilcoxes, Sargeants, and Coxes all knew one another. Perhaps Minnie Wilcox, who knew Eckley and Charles Coxe, introduced her Southern friend Lizzie Sinkler to Charles Brinton Coxe. In the following letter Charles Brinton Coxe asked Charles Sinkler for Lizzie's hand in marriage.

Philadelphia, September 23, 1869

My Dear Mr. Sinkler,

It is not in my power to express in words the great happiness your letter received on Monday, gave me. It was especially gratifying that you and Mrs. Sinkler gave your unqualified consent and approval. I fully appreciated the very delicate position in which you were placed by an utter stranger asking you to give the future of your daughter into his hands. I know you had to rely on the judgment of those of your family living here, and I feel sure you will never have cause to regret that you did so. For my devotion to your daughter through life will prove I am worthy of the trust and that my love is very genuine and sincere. Miss Lizzie has not yet decided exactly when she will leave for the South, being dependent on Miss Chestnut's movements, but I shall follow her a few days after as there are numerous things you will want to know about me and my affairs, which

27. Minnie Wilcox to Elizabeth Sinkler, Vances Ferry, P.O., South Carolina, January 18, 1867, letter in the possession of author LeClercq.

can be better explained in a personal interview, than in numerous letters. I hope also to begin an acquaintance which will soon grow into an affectionate relationship. Can I send my love to Mrs. Sinkler and the little girls? Tell Mary I intend writing to her in a few days.

Yours very sincerely,
Charles B. Coxe[28]

Lizzie was not the only Sinkler to fall in love in the fall of 1869. Her brother Wharton, who had graduated from the University of Pennsylvania Medical School in 1868, had dated Ella Brock for several years. In October 1869 Kate Wharton, the wife of Emily's brother Henry Wharton wrote Emily about Wharton's exciting news:

Chestnut Hill Monday Evening, October 25, 1869[29]

My dearest Emily,
. . . What is the world coming to! . . . I don't think I ever saw Henry more surprised. The fact is that I was too for the moment, for although I long ago made up my mind as to Wharton, one can never tell about things, and I thought it quite likely to go on just in this way for a long while. But I am really so rejoiced and delighted about it. I feel indeed that we all ought to congratulate each other. Wharton's wife must be always very near to me and for her to be a person to whom I am already attached and of whom I think so highly as I do of Ella, is really a pleasure. . . . She has very noble traits of character and very deep and true feelings too. . . . But my dear Emily, I do feel so much about you that I scarcely know how to express myself in words. I know what it must be to you, for you to have two such shocks seems really too much. . . . . And it is too hard to have them away from you! . . . I had a note from Lizzie today saying that she is going with Mrs. Chestnut who is to leave Baltimore on Friday. Henry and I will probably go on to Baltimore with her on Thursday. . . . Most Affectionately yours, Kate Wharton

28. Charles B. Coxe to Charles Sinkler, September 23, 1869, letter in the possession of author LeClercq.
29. Kate Wharton to Emily Sinkler, Chestnut Hill, October 25, 1869, letter in the possession of author LeClercq.

As Kate Wharton intimated it must have been difficult for Charles and Emily Sinkler to have their two beloved older children, Lizzie and Wharton, living in the North and marrying Philadelphians. The Whartons, Sinklers, and Coxes celebrated the marriage of Lizzie and Charles on June 14, 1870. In 1872 Wharton Sinkler and Ella Brock were married in Philadelphia.

Lizzie made it a lifelong habit to eschew discussion of the South's role in the Civil War. She was not one to relive old battles and to remember lost honor. She moved on with her life very quickly and made herself a contributing member of the Drifton community.

One letter remains of the many she must have written Emily, and in it we see Lizzie's easy adaptability and happiness with her new role as Mrs. Charles Brinton Coxe. She was cooking, entertaining, and enjoying life in Drifton but missed her mother terribly. The Aunt Kate she refers to is Katharine Johnstone Brinley Wharton, married to Emily's brother Henry Wharton (1827–1880).

Drifton, August 29, 1870

My dearest Mama,

I have been so miserable about you since Friday for I have not heard from you since today week and your letter was dated as far back as the 18th, and all your letters have come so regularly that you cannot wonder it makes me uneasy. Since writing the above I have been a good deal relieved in mind by a telegram from Wharton. On Saturday when I felt so wretchedly at not hearing from you Charley telegraphed to him to know what was the date of his last letter, and no answer came from him till just now, owing to his being out at Chestnut Hill.[30] He says his last date was the 19th but Aunt Kate got a letter on Saturday and all were well. He doesn't mention the date of it but I think it must have been later. Still I shall most anxiously look for a letter from you today. I was almost as bad as you in my imaginings for I took an idea some of you had typhoid fever. By the bye I see Dr. Pancoast[31] says most cases of typhoid come from bad feather

30. Chestnut Hill is a suburb of Philadelphia where Ella Brock and Wharton Sinkler lived.

31. Lizzie is probably referring to Philadelphia physician Joseph Pancoast (1805–1882). Lizzie's observation is interesting in that she either read the medical

beds. As I feel so much cheered in mind I can tell you about our visit from Bishop Stevens which I must begin with quite a funny story of McCoy.

I wrote a note to Mr. Walker, the minister at Eckley asking him and the Bishop to dine with us yesterday after church, and told Charley he had better tell McCoy to tell him who it was from as I was sure he would not know who E. A. Coxe was. But Charley forgot to do it and McCoy brought back an answer in a blank envelope and beginning "Dear Mr. Coxe." The funny part is though that McCoy said with an air of triumph "he asked me who the note was from and I told him sure that's none of my business, and then he asked who I would give his answer to and I said I'll give it to them that sent me, so concluded McCoy, grinning with delight, "he got no satisfaction out of me." The Bishop had quite a crowded audience at the schoolhouse yesterday afternoon and preached an excellent clear sermon just adapted to them and then came back to dinner and was very agreeable. He immediately said he must claim fellowship with me on the score of being a Georgian and spoke in a very warm way of the South saying he could not stand going back there and seeing the changes. It seems he is a Bostonian originally but lived in Georgia very long and graduated in medicine in Charleston.[32] He spoke of knowing Uncle Frank very well and told Eckley before he got here that he knew the "Sinklers," I suppose meaning you and Papa. He admired our house very much but seemed to have no fancy for the coal region and dirty little coal towns and wanted to know if I had seen the place before I agreed to live here and was inclined to be very facetious when I said I had not only seen it but liked it exceedingly.

We had Becky to dinner too and a very nice dinner. First we had okra soup, then leg of mutton, chicken with cream sauce, baked tomatoes, eggplant, sweet and white potatoes, and beets. Then for another course macaroni, tomato salad and rice croquets, and for dessert ice cream, cut up peaches, trifle, Italian cream and cake and after dinner coffee. What do you think of the Bishop having a baby three weeks off? We had a wood fire last night, the third morning in succession. I must stop now to write to Wharton as I fear I have made him uneasy by the telegram. How I hope and pray

---

literature or discussed medical topics, perhaps with her brother Wharton Sinkler or S. Weir Mitchell, who treated her for exhaustion after the Civil War.

32. The Medical College of South Carolina in Charleston was established in 1824.

I may have a good news from you today. With much love to all your devoted Lizzie.

The young couple was married only the requisite nine months when
Lizzie gave birth to Charles Brinton Coxe, Jr. By May 20, 1871, she was re-
covering from childbirth with an attentive husband at her side. Charley
again wrote his old friend John Cadwalader:

> How kind and sympathetic you have been to us. Lizzie has so often spo-
> ken of you and when your flowers came yesterday it touched her very,
> very much. I had to unpack them along side of her bed. . . . You know
> how sweetly she arranges flowers and it was a great interest to her to direct
> me. . . . I had to take them out over and over again before they were to her
> satisfaction. It is always a joy to us when we can get her to take interest in
> anything. . . . Lizzie had last night the longest continuous sleep yet and is
> steadily improving. The Dr. intends keeping her in bed a few days longer
> but allows her now to have some decent food. She was speaking of your
> wife yesterday with so much love and affection. I did not know before
> that her love was so tender and strong.[33]

This first baby of Charles and Lizzie was to die in infancy. The young couple spent the fall in Drifton. Life in Drifton, a small mining village, was slow
paced. The Coxe brothers—Charles, Aleck, and Eckley—were busy setting
up coal mining operations that were yet to flourish. Their wives were pre-
occupied with having children, keeping house, and being mothers. Philadelphia was only a three-day train ride to the South, and with daily trains
the young Coxes were undoubtedly frequently there doing business and
staying with friends and family.

Charley's personal friendship with John Cadwalader continued. The war
letters reflected a young, insecure, homesick youth longing for the support, companionship, and friendship of his Penn classmate and fraternity
brother John Cadwalader. By 1872 both men were married with burgeon-
ing families, and their bond of friendship had become less personal.

On May 31, 1872, Charley and Lizzie produced another young son,
whom they named Eckley Brinton Coxe Jr. The baby was born twelve
months after their first baby. Lizzie with her petite frame may have struggled with two pregnancies so closely spaced.

---

33. Coxe to Cadwalader, Drifton, May 20, 1871, Cadwalader-JCJS.

In a letter dated July 2, 1872, Charley wrote John telling him of the events passing in Drifton. There was mention of their past friendship, of the birth of young Eckley, and a visit from Emily Wharton Sinkler and Lizzie's younger sisters and brother. The letter concluded with a plea for a visit.

Drifton
July 2, 1872

Dear John,

I have just been reading over your letter and it shames me that I have let so many days go by without answering it especially as at the time yours came I was thinking of writing to tell you how sorry I had been to miss you last week we were in town. I was at your office several times and instead of seeing your sweet face, saw that oddity you have there to whom it never struck me to leave my name and of course you never knew what you missed. I did hear you thought I was a little "put out" but dear old John those "put out" days have long gone. My affection for you dear fellow is of a better order now for I would not doubt your line, no matter how much appearances might be against you unless you told me yourself and of that I have no fear.

Life has progressed with us most favorably since coming up here. The baby continues splendid and since last Monday when Mrs. Doran left, we have had him in our room. I had looked forward to weary nights but I must do the little fellow justice, he has behaved most decorously, not troubling me in the slightest degree and Lizzie not more so than could be expected under the circumstances. Long may he continue so. Lizzie declares and I believe her that the baby is a joy and a comfort but as yet I have not been able to rise to that high state of happiness about him. However, I sincerely hope I may for the boy is here and we must keep him and in all fairness I should have the joy of him as long as I must have the trouble and discomfort.

Mrs. Sinkler and the children leave here tomorrow for Narragansett, but will return to us for a couple of weeks before leaving for the South. I am very sorry they are going and all of them prefer remaining here but Mr. Sinkler has written for them to go and he may join them there, altho it is extremely doubtful. Lizzie and I will be alone until they return and the hotel is very quiet without Aleck and his family. Why won't you take pity on us and come up next Sunday. If you could not come in the morning train, we could easily meet you in Hazleton by the afternoon train. You know that Lizzie and I have a very nice pair of horses and a wagon of our own which is a great comfort. Heretofore we were dependent on others for all our needs and drives. . . . Do come next Sunday. It would be such a real pleasure to have you. Love from both of us to your family, especially dear little Helen.

Your friend, CBC

In close succession, Lizzie was to experience two deeply personal tragedies, the death of her husband and the death of her beloved mother. On January 3, 1873, Charles Brinton Coxe died in Cairo, Egypt. It is unknown why he and Lizzie had suddenly visited Egypt. Perhaps it was for health reasons, as Egyptian winters were known to be dry and sunny, and many sojourned there to recuperate from various illnesses. Or perhaps Charles's interest in Egypt was scholarly, as he had been a student at the University of Pennsylvania when a small group undertook another translation of the Rosetta Stone.[34] Lizzie brought his body home to Philadelphia, and he was buried in the Woodlands Cemetery, where she and Eckley Jr. were later buried.

Lizzie, who had always been a mother to her younger siblings, Charlie, Mary, and Carrie, was soon to become the mother, in fact, to Emily and Charles's small brood. On Ash Wednesday, February 10, 1875, Emily was thrown from a buggy while returning home to Belvidere from church service at The Rocks Church. Lizzie's sisters, Mary Wharton Sinkler and Caroline Sidney Sinkler, were young—seventeen and fifteen, respectively. Lizzie took her responsibility to these younger sisters seriously. Carrie came to live with her, and together they purchased a home at 1604 Locust Street in Philadelphia. They became inseparable traveling companions, always including Lizzie's young son, Eckley Brinton Coxe Jr.

There is no written record of the next twenty years of Lizzie and young Eckley's life. During that time the Coxe family fortunes grew from coal mining. Eckley went to school in Philadelphia and Drifton. Lizzie developed her spirit of adventure and her wanderlust. Her early travels with her mother between North and South had made her an intrepid traveler. When

---

34. Although the Rosetta Stone was found in Rashid (Rosetta), Egypt, in 1799, it was not "translated" until 1822. Since the stone featured text in three alphabets, it served as the key to deciphering Egyptian hieroglyphics.

the written record and story of her life resume, the twosome plus family members are indefatigable globetrotters.

In 1895 Lizzie and son Eckley built a forty-five room residence in the Pennsylvania Hills in Drifton, which they called Windy Hill. This became Lizzie's Northern home and the center of her life. The house had a large library as well as a ballroom. Lizzie was attended by well-trained Irish servants. Lizzie's personal maid was named Hannah, and Kendel was the coachman. There were gardeners, valets, and cooks.

The house at Windy Hill was nestled in an extensive, professionally designed garden.[35] The highly waxed floors reflected vases of perennial phlox and blue hydrangeas from the garden. The phlox gave a fragrance to the entire house. In the living room there was a Steinway grand piano. As in her early days at Belvidere, Lizzie played classical music in the evenings, delighting parties of friends and family.

The dining room was large, with an elegant table that could seat eighteen people. The tablecloths were of beautiful damask with intricately and exquisitely stitched monograms. Lizzie carried on the culinary traditions she had learned at Belvidere, adding delicacies available only in the North, such as fresh raspberries.

Like her mother, Lizzie was an avid gardener. The lovely and welcoming house at Windy Hill was situated amongst handsome trees and looked out over the surrounding hills. It had a broad piazza across the front of the house with wide glass French doors. All the windows had diamond-shaped mullions, which gave the interior of the house an iridescent glow. After breakfast the ladies assembled on the broad front piazza. One of them would read aloud the morning papers and then progress to a biography or a novel. The others would embroider or mend.

The garden at Windy Hill had a handsome downhill vista as seen from the broad piazza. The vista was fifty feet wide and led downhill three hundred feet with steps at intervals of fifteen feet. At the bottom was a lovely pool with a thirty-foot jet of water. At right angles there were broad lawns. On one side there was a tennis court and on the other a rose arbor with comfortable chairs and benches. Lizzie especially loved her fragrant phlox

---

35. This description of the house and gardens at Windy Hill is drawn from recollections of Emily Fishburne Whaley, the mother of the author, who visited Windy Hill on many occasions.

garden, which was near the broad front piazza. In the center of that garden was a special cherub fountain that made a gurgling splash.

Like her mother, Emily, Lizzie lived between North and South. After the death of Emily she continued to visit her father at Belvidere until his death on March 28, 1894. Lizzie continued her visits to Belvidere every spring, staying with her younger brother Charlie and his wife Anne Wickham Porcher Sinkler,[36] who continued to operate Belvidere as a cotton plantation. Lizzie's Southern home, Belvidere was important throughout her life. Lizzie became the link to the Sinklers in the South, sending Christmas packages. Her yearly visits were usually timed to the Easter season, late March and early April. She would come loaded with new Easter dresses and hats for her young nieces. The Belvidere house was filled with swamp Easter lilies for this occasion. Charlie and Anne's three daughters, Anne, Emily, and Caroline, spent long summers with Lizzie at Windy Hill. Lizzie's brother Wharton had married Ella Brock[37] of Philadelphia, and they had four sons, Wharton, Jack, Charles, and Deas, and two daughters, Julia and Elsie. They were frequent visitors at Belvidere and at Windy Hill. Lizzie's sister Mary Wharton Sinkler had married Charles Stevens of Northhampton Plantation. They moved to Lewisfield Plantation on the Cooper River with their children, Elizabeth, Laura, and Henry. They also visited Lizzie at Windy Hill. The Belvidere Sinklers spent many happy holidays at Windy Hill with Lizzie and Eckley.

Lizzie and Eckley spent spring and summer at Windy Hill. However, during the cold and foreboding winter months they traveled by steamer to the warm old world ports of the Mediterranean. The first of these many voyages was to Algiers sometime prior to 1894.

36. Anne Wickham Porcher Sinkler (1860–1919).

37. Before Wharton Sinkler married Ella Brock in 1872, his manservant Mingo Rivers dictated this note to Emily Sinkler to be given to Miss Brock: "I will say to you dear Miss that I am very glad you have found my respectable boy Dr. Wharton Sinkler—who he & me have traveled together from his youth up & I can say he was always respected & affectionate. In times of frolickins of other young gentlemen he never done so, but would take his little Testament & go apart & call Mingo. And I would say to him how different you are from other young men. I am praying to God that you & he will be happy always. And I am hoping that God will bless you and that we will meet some day—From your affectionate friend Mingo Rivers" (Sinkler Family Papers, undated letter, 11/388/8. Sinkler Family Papers. South Carolina History Society, Charleston, South Carolina).

CHAPTER TWO

A Stop in Algiers, 1893

The route from America to the Old World often began with a stop in Algeria. In this letter from Algiers, Lizzie and Eck were enjoying the beauty of French-dominated Algeria. This was the height of colonial empire. The Mediterranean was a secure inland sea for traveling Americans. The steamships were large and comfortable. The destinations were French- or British-controlled. There was every accustomed convenience, from English chemist shops and English tailors to English churches and fine, well-staffed hotels with beautiful gardens. Cooks Steam line had offices in Algiers. There were English hairdressers, English-made piano stores, English cigar stores, riding schools where ladies were taught and escorted, steam dyers and cleaners (where English was spoken), English shirts readymade or made to order, with scarves and foulards of all kinds, millinery stores with a large assortment of hats for ladies and children (advertising English spoken), even a store called Old England at 4 Boulevard de la Republique, Algiers, where there were ladies' tailors for dresses, riding, hunting, and tennis suits. Indeed, everything was available to make the English, American, or French visitor totally happy.[1]

It was extraordinary that Lizzie and her entourage of young ladies were totally comfortable in a society with such different cultural mores. Women were treated like slaves. "The position of the Arab woman in Algeria is theoretically much preferable to that of her sex in Morocco or Turkey. The strictly equitable nature of the French rule forbids her being treated with harshness or sold into slavery; but practically she is not much better off

---

1. George W. Harris, *The Practical Guide to Algiers,* 9th ed. (London: George Philip & Son, 1899), 5–74 (advertising section).

than in other Oriental countries. She is the victim of a stupid and brutalizing social code, founded on and bound up in a religion whose theory is pure, but whose practice is barbarous. She is either condemned or maltreated; a toy to the rich, a beast of burden to the poor."[2] Why indeed was Algiers so popular with the well-to-do traveler? Climate and health were two popular explanations. Individuals with bronchitis, asthma, afflictions of the heart, Bright's disease, and pulmonary consumption flocked to Algiers because of a winter climate that was dry and warm. "According to recent statistics, the proportion of deaths from pulmonary consumption among the European population of Algeria during a period of six years, was one in forty, while the proportion of deaths from the same disease in Paris and London was one in five."[3]

Lizzie and Eckley began what was to become a lifelong passion for travel in each other's company. Lizzie wrote to her sister Caroline Sidney Sinkler (1860–1948), fondly called Carrie and sometimes Cad. Carrie lived with Lizzie at 1604 Locust Street in Philadelphia. She also had her own estate at the Highlands in Ambler, Pennsylvania. Lizzie often brought her nieces and nephews with her on these travels. On this trip she included Julia Ursula Sinkler (b. 1872), the oldest daughter of Wharton Sinkler (1845–1910). Wharton, Lizzie's brother, was a prominent neurologist in Philadelphia, and had been a protégé of S. Weir Mitchell and other famous medical men.

Hotel Continental

Mustapha Superieur, Alger[4]

Tuesday, January 16 [sometime prior to 1894]

2. Ibid., 16.

3. Ibid., 1–7. "Algiers does not offer the same distractions as Nice, Cannes, or the winter resorts of Italy. The chief attractions of Algiers are its climatic advantages. Apart from the Municipal Theatre, . . . there are no local festivities worthy of the name. . . . Visitors to Algiers should not miss viewing the sacrifice of the hen which takes place in the winter, every Wednesday morning. . . . The Governor General's ball, which is given about the 15th of March, is a very fashionable gathering; it offers to the visitor the means of studying the local society of Algiers, and . . . it affords the facility of contemplating the Arab Sheiks and Aghas in the full glare of their dashing costumes. The Caids, with their red burnouses are there in overwhelming numbers" (65).

4. Mustapha Superieur was a comfortable English- and French-dominated suburb of Algiers. "Persons who intend spending more than one or two nights in

Dearest Carrie,

This picture does not give you a very good idea of our hotel, for it looks so dark around while all is colour and brightness. The middle little excrescence is our balcony from which we have the enchanting view I told you of and when we stand on it and look down we see several Moors and 2 Spaniards spreading out on the white tiled terrace their showy wares and the clusters of orange and lemon trees which border the terrace and drop their golden fruit on it.[5] The Spaniard's costumes are truly gorgeous—just like the Matadors,[6] and by the bye there is to be a real Spanish bullfight

---

Algiers are recommended to stop at one of the hotels at Mustapha Superieur which is within easy access (2 m.) of the town by omnibus every half-hour or by carriage (3f.). Mustapha Superieur is well situated on the slopes of the hills S. of Algiers amongst gardens and pine woods and commands extensive views; and being at a considerable elevation above the sea, it has the great advantage of being fresher and more healthy than the town." The Hotel Continental et D'Orient advertised itself as a first-class hotel with the following amenities: "Full south, Splendid View. Four Acres of Gardens, Tennis Court. English Billiard Table, Calorifere, Excellent Drainage, Hydraulic Lift, Ascenseur. Omnibus on Arrival of Steamers" (R. Lambert Playfair, *Handbook for Travellers in Algeria and Tunis* [London: John Murray, 1895], 106, index, 4).

5. The view from the Hotel Continental must have been special. "Algiers, the ancient Icosium, is situated on the western shore of the bay of the same name, 500 m. S. of Marseilles. The town, which is triangular in form, is built on a slop of the Sahel, the name given to a chain of hills running along the coast for a considerable distance towards the w. The view, when approaching it from the sea, is most beautiful. It appears from a distance like a succession of dazzling white steps or terraces rising from the water, which contrasting with the bright green background of the Sahel, explains the origin of the Arab comparison of Algiers to a diamond set in an emerald frame" (ibid., 93).

6. "Here may be seen the embroiderer at work with his gold and silver thread, the shoemaker with kid slippers of every colour and variety, the pedagogue with his school of young Moors, the worker in gold and silver, the barber shaving Moorish heads or chins, and the cafes where the natives sit cross legged drinking coffee, and while away their time in smoking and playing draughts. . . . But perhaps what most strikes the traveler from Europe on first walking through the city is the variety and picturesqueness of costumes he meets in the streets. French soldiers and officers, Zouaves and Turcos, with their smart uniforms; the Jew with dark-coloured turban, jacket and sash, blue stockings and shoes; the Moor in smartly embroidered jacket, full short trousers, and white stockings; bare-legged Arabs, wrapped in their white bournous; Mozabites with their coats of many colours; Negroes from the

soon which Eck and Ob are going to, and they are also going to a horrible exhibition of fire eaters on Thursday night in which they run daggers in their eyes and do horrid things.[7] It is a great comfort to have Ob to go with him to such things as he does not know any young men.

I think Julia quite misses all her beaux of the steamer and that her greatest enjoyment so far has been the voyage which to me was such misery. We are getting quite sociable however with 2 very lively young Germans here who fancy they speak splendid English.[8] The English people here are exactly like in novels, especially the elderly women with sniffy manners and wonderful clothes, but there are dressy stout mothers with pallid pathetic sons who go to my heart. And next to us are two American sisters who talk French volubly and are thorough wanderers. Poor Eck sits at the head of the table with me on one side and a nice old Swiss gentleman and his daughter on the other who talk French to me and German to each other. Bad as my French is we contrive to laugh and talk a good deal and Eck thinks it very trying.

But fancy how galling for him that Julia or I have to accompany him always to the photographers and the cigar store even. We drink Algerian wine and St. Evian water, and Ob says they give him wine at 6 cents a bottle and brandy free in his black coffee and on Sunday a bouquet and a book to read. We have had a little wood fire once, but now in the fire place is a pitcher with a great bunch of wild flowers we got on our drive yesterday, and on the table a brown jug with a huge bunch of violets.

Soudan; Spaniards and Maltese, all jostle one another in the crowded streets; while Moorish women, dressed in white, with full trousers, slippers and their faces covered to the eyes, mingle with ladies in fashionable modern toilets and with Jewesses whose jaws are bound with a muslin handkerchief and whose straight silk robes reach from the neck to the slippered feet" (ibid., 96).

7. Ob is an unidentifiable friend of Eck's.

8. Algiers was indeed social. "The great desideratum at Algiers has always been some place where English and Americans might meet together, and enjoy something like social life. Thanks to the public spirit of a few of the principal residents a club of unusual excellence has been established in the Villa de royer at Mustapha superieur. It is situated in beautiful grounds, with lawn tennis courts, and is abundantly supplied with current literature. Entertainments of various kinds are given every Monday during the season" (R. Lambert Playfair, *Handbook for Travellers in Algeria and Tunis* [London: John Murray, 1895], 102).

These two mornings we have had our light breakfast in the café and gone down town in the hotel bus that goes at 9½ and returned at 12 in time for lunch. So far we have only walked about the French streets and squares and bought photos, gloves and patisserie of wonderful and delightful kinds and gone to the Post Office and tried to squeeze letters out of them, and been all the time followed by little Arab beggars in tatters but with fascinating little faces. If you give one a copper the crowd increases till you are perfectly worn out. If you frown and shake your fist they laugh and make funny faces. Little wretches of about 4 pursue the omnibus at full speed in the most crowded streets until your nerves are worn out.

I can give you no idea of the picturesque variety in the streets—but it is really fascinating. The French Gouaves in their bright uniforms and the officers are too magnificent and ride such beautiful Arab horses. There are the horridly dirty Arabs and then fine stately looking Moors in beautiful costumes and girls enveloped in snow-white thin sheets with only their eyes showing and the fullest baggiest white trousers you can imagine. The donkeys are too delightful and Eck is going to bring home a collection of their portraits.

We had a very beautiful drive yesterday. The roads are very fine though it is so hilly. We passed many beautiful villas—Moorish—with enchanting gardens full of flowers. They have stone walls but many carved arches in them showing fountains and terraces and little tiled kiosks covered with roses and unknown flowering vines. We drove to the Jardins d'Essai, which are wonderfully beautiful.[9] There are avenues of gigantic palms and others still more beautiful of majestic graceful bamboo arching overhead, and as long a vista as the eye can take in. I had no idea there was such vegetation.

---

9. "Turning now to the W., we reach the Jardin d'Essai, a garden of about 200 hectares in extent. This was commenced in 1832 and while it remained in the hands of Government it was kept up with great care but at a great expense; . . . still it is a delightful promenade, and it contains a most interesting collection of plants, both in the open air and in greenhouses. Ornamental plants are cultivated in great numbers and exported to the principal cities of Europe. The avenues of planes, palms, bamboos, and magnolias are especially worthy of notice. On the opposite side of the road on the slope of the hill is another portion of the same garden, principally devoted to Australian plants such as eucalyptus, araucarias, acacias, etc. The whole crowned by a wood of Canary pines" (ibid., 108).

On Sunday we went to the English church which is small but beautiful and very pathetic.[10] It is all covered inside with slabs and tiles of the loveliest red and pink Algerian marbles and many of these are inscribed with names and memorials. On one side are all the Englishmen and some Americans who died in captivity here in the pirate times and those who were killed fighting the Moors, and the names of 2 merchants who gave all their fortunes to ransom others out of slavery. On the other side there are still more touching little inscriptions of those who have evidently died far from home in modern times. The old English clergyman with a velvet skull-cap and the young one with a red Oxford hood and delightful intonation and the volunteer choir with nice soft voices and familiar Epiphany hymns, we enjoyed all of.

It seemed to me so long since I had been to church and so impossible to imagine it was only 3 weeks since Xmas. We expect to leave here in the *Normannia* on the 27th for Genoa. It stops a few hours I believe at Naples. We expect to spend 2 days in Genoa and have written to engage rooms for Feb. 1st at the Hotel Californie Cannes.

I do hope and pray you are all well. How I long to hear from you, no words can tell. Give my dear love to Papa and the others, and do send this to Mary.[11] I will write to her next.

Your devoted, Lil

10. "The church of the Holy Trinity, at the Port d'Isly, was erected in 1870 by subscription of the winter visitors. . . . The building, though not very attractive outside is one of the most interesting of its kind out of England. A dado or podium has been erected all round the church, with a more elaborate reredos behind the altar, composed of alternate slabs of different kinds of marbles and breccias, framed in bands of giallo antico and breccia dorata, surmounted by smaller tablets of rose coloured marble. In the nave and baptistery these contain memorial inscriptions. . . . The walls on the north, south, and east sides of the nave above this podium are entirely covered with rich marbles, so arranged as to be available for memorial inscriptions. . . . All the windows, eighteen in number, have been filled in with stained glass, generally with memorial brasses attached to commemorate historical personages. . . . The large circular window at the west end is in memory of the English who perished in captivity during the time of the Deys. . . . The decoration of the east end is particularly beautiful; the whole of the walls and the reveals of the windows in the apse and choir have been covered with marble mosaics" (ibid., 97, 98).

11. Papa was Charles Sinkler (1818–1894). Thus this letter was written sometime prior to 1894. Mary Wharton Sinkler (1857–1934) was Lizzie's younger sister and the mother of Elizabeth Allen Stevens, Lizzie's frequent traveling companion.

CHAPTER THREE

Egypt, Greece, and Italy, 1895

In the winter of 1895 Lizzie was traveling with her sister Carrie, a friend, Oliver, and an in-law, Mary Jane Brinton.[1] Her party was headed to Cairo, Luxor, Athens, Trieste, and Rome. Her journal and letters from that trip were full of enthusiasm for the sights. But she worried about Eckley when he was away on a trip to see the temple at Abu Simbel. She was proud of his ingenuity in avoiding the strike of cab drivers in Athens. She was admiring of his good looks as he dressed for a fancy ball at the Khedive's palace. Eck was her constant companion and closest friend. They traveled on the Rameses, one of the steamships in the Cook Nile Service fleet.[2] Lizzie

---

1. The exact relationship between Lizzie Coxe and Mary Jane Brinton is not known, but since Charles Brinton Coxe's mother was a Brinton, it is believed that Mary Jane was a young niece or cousin through marriage.

2. "The itineraries of these steamers are planned in the special interest of sightseers, and for travelers of a social and gregarious disposition there can be no more comfortable and luxurious method of doing the temples and ruins of Upper Egypt. One of the fine saloon steamers of Messrs. Cook leaves Cairo every Tuesday at 10 A.M. For a twenty days' voyage to Luxor and Assouan and back the fare, which includes all expenses, board, conveyance to or from the temples, backsheesh, service of dragoman, medical attendance . . . is 50 pounds. . . . The famous triad of Rameses steamers are reserved for the regular service. These saloon steamers are perhaps the most luxurious and best appointed river steamers in the world. They are, however, apt to be very crowded—the most popular vessel, Rameses the Great, having had every berth taken during the last six seasons." The steamships were 220 feet long, had steel hulls and 500-horsepower engines, bathrooms with hot and cold water, electricity, ice machines, reading saloons, and an English doctor to accompany each vessel (E. A. Reynolds-Ball, *Cairo of To-Day: A Practical Guide to Cairo and its Environs* [London: Adam and Charles Black, 1899], 170–71).

enjoyed the cool breezes of the Nile and remained on-board when she was not feeling up to traveling over desert sands. The trip ended at Shepheard's Hotel in Cairo, a watering spot for British and American visitors to Egypt. Following is Lizzie's journal entry for this trip. It is untitled.

There were many interesting people on board, and we found it a comfortable way of traveling. Each of us had our own stateroom, containing every comfort, electric lights and screens, and the most deft and well trained Arab stewards in their long white gowns, red sashes and fezzes to wait upon us. The big salons and spaces for sitting on deck on all sides were charming, and the meals were generally excellent, especially the Greek pastry cooks' desserts. Of course we got rather tired of the goat meat they called "mutton," and the skinny pigeons, that shortly before they were cooked had been flying around the mosques and the Cross and Blackwell's tinned butter, but that mattered little.

After dinner every evening, Raschad, our magnificently dressed Arab dragoman, clapped his hands and walked between the tables, giving us the program of where we would stop and what we would see the next day; and entreating us not to get off the boat in the morning until he had arranged for the donkeys for our party.[3] We tied up to the bank near some village every night, and the fragrance of the sweet bean flowers, the creaking of the sakiyeh wheels, and the sad but enchanting songs of the Arabs filled the nights.

The most exciting scene always when we stopped to visit some old temple or town was when Raschad and Mohammed, a huge black assistant dragoman, went on shore and looked over all the donkeys that had been brought down for the party.[4] The transaction was guarded by the

3. As Lizzie noted, a dragoman, or Arab guide, was essential to any visiting party. "In Murray's Guide a useful list of well-recommended dragomans is given." One expected a dragoman to make all arrangements. For example: "No doubt the most satisfactory way of visiting the great Pyramid Field . . . is to devote three or four consecutive days to their exploration, and camp out. Any Cairo dragoman would arrange this and would provide everything (tents, food, transport, etc.) for a party of not less than three at about 2 pounds per day per head (ibid., 19, 141).

4. "Conveyances.—Donkeys.—The donkey-boys usually expect at least 5 piastres for half a day and 10 or 12 piastres for the whole day. This should include baksheesh. There is an understanding among the guides and donkey-boys on either

Zaptean, or native policemen, who in their skin tight dark green
uniforms had only the red fez and terrible rhinoceros korbash like
their Arab brethren.[5]

Sometimes we had nice Arab donkey boys who were very amusing.
Once when we made the long hot ride through the burning sands to
Saqqara, my boy Achmed, produced an orange for me from the inside
of his one blue cotton garment, and not long after, brought out a skull
from the same receptacle, which he said he had found in a tomb.[6] Frequently little Arab girls ran along by our sides for miles, carrying jugs
of water on their heads.

It would be tiresome for me to try to describe these wonderful visits
to the temples, the memories of which throng to my mind with intense
interest. I think perhaps I remember Dendera with the greatest pleasure—
beginning with the little copper-colored naked boys with garlands of
green leaves hung over their shoulders.[7] The luncheons brought from

---

side of the river, which prevents their being taken from Luxor to Thebes or vice
versa" (ibid., 186).

5. A korbash was the whip carried at this time by police and officials—as much
a symbol of their authority as it was a flail against the truculent.

6. Saqqara is a plateau overlooking the ancient capital of Memphis with over
fifteen royal pyramids. It served as a necropolis site for the early dynasties of Egypt.
It is over six kilometers long. The famous Step Pyramid of Djoser (2630–2622
B.C.E.) is located on the northernmost region. It was designed by Imhotep, known
as the inventor of the art of building with hewn stone. The pyramid of Wenis
(2356–2323 B.C.E.), the last king of the Fifth Dynasty, is also located there. A large
complex of underground rock-cut chambers has also been located under the east
side of the pyramid of Wenis. The walls of the interior of this pyramid are inscribed with the Pyramid Texts, a collection of spells designed to help the deceased
king in the netherworld. Around these royal tombs were many belonging to
nobles, including the tomb of Ty, an official of the Fifth Dynasty, with its inscriptions and reliefs, which are elaborate depictions of daily life and mortuary legends.
The southern region of Saqqara contains the pyramid of Pepy II, called Mennefer-
Mare, which lent its name to the entire region, including Memphis, the Greek form
of the Egyptian Menfi (John Baines and Jaromir Malek, *Atlas of Ancient Egypt*
[New York: Facts on File, 1980], 142–51).

7. Lizzie and her party would have gone by steamer and then by donkey to the
temple at Dendera. The temple was a quarter of an hour's ride from the mooring
place on the river at the town of Qena. This beautiful and well-preserved temple
belongs to a late Ptolemaic period. The inscriptions on the walls of the Temple

the boats on the backs of camels by the stewards, and eaten in the lofty halls of some great temple, the pillars decorated with the life story of the battle scenes of the Pharoahs were among our pleasantest experiences. In going through the temples and palaces on the Nile, one sees everywhere colossal statues of Rameses the Second—young, smiling, and all-powerful, the crowns of upper and lower Egypt on his head, and grasping the key of life in his hand. Then, at the museum in Cairo, one sees his mummy in a glass case—his dried brown features still showing his strong character; but now at the mercy of every staring tourist.[8] I always think there is something very touching in hearing that after the tombs of the kings were discovered, and the mummies carried down the Nile on large barges to be placed in the Museum, that all the villages along the river gathered on the banks and sang loud laments and funeral songs, perhaps the same as those used when they were buried thousands of years ago.

When we arrived at Luxor, Eckley found that a small party was going on up to the second cataract in a smaller steamboat, and determined he must go to see Abou Simbel and Abou Seir. So he left us for the week's trip, taking Oliver who was keen for the adventure. We stayed down at the Luxor hotel which was very attractive, surrounded by a garden which was kept irrigated by one of the sakiyeh from the Nile. It seems to me there were flowers from every clime in that garden, including the purple, very fragrant "Pride of India." But the week he was away was very long, especially as I had a great fright. A boat load of tourists came up from Cairo one evening, among them the Dolans, who said they had intended going up to the second cataract, but a message had been received from General

---

of Hathor remain remarkably intact as the temple was buried under sand until the nineteenth century. There is an astronomical ceiling of great beauty as well as a large relief on the exterior wall showing Cleopatra making offerings to Hathor. Caesarion, her son by Julius Caesar, stands in front of her burning incense (E. A. Reynolds-Ball, *Cairo of To-Day: A Practical Guide to Cairo and its Environs* [London: Adam and Charles Black, 1899], 182). The astronomical ceiling at Dendera has been removed and is today in the Louvre Museum.

8. In 1895 the National Museum of Antiquities was housed in the Palace of Ghizerah, once the harem of Khedive Ismail. There were ninety rooms with exhibits arranged chronologically. Lizzie went there to see the mummy of Rameses II. The mummies were discovered by Brugsch Bey in 1881 at Dar-el-Bahari, near Thebes. Rameses II is described as "the Pharaoh of the Oppression" (ibid., 83).

Kitchener to allow no one to proceed farther than Luxor—as the Mahdi was attacking his troops and fighting was probably going on. To my intense relief, I presently received a telegram from Eckley, saying they were quite safe, and on their way down the river. Nevertheless I spent most of my time, like David, sitting on a curious seat above the gate, watching the river for a returning boat. The accounts of their excursion were deeply interesting. General Kitchener gave them permission to go up to the rock of Abou Seir with a guard of eighteen of his Soudanese camel corps.[9] The eighteen tourists were mounted on small donkeys; but after starting they offered the soldiers large baksheesh to exchange mounts with them. For eighteen miles they rode through the burning desert, carrying the soldiers' rifles, but enjoying the excitement and the whole trip.

Oliver was very ill at Luxor after they came back, and when we again reached Cairo we were very glad to get the first cabins possible on a Russian steamer sailing from Alexandria to the Pireas. However, this was a very troublesome trip; for when we got on board the steamer at Alexandria, Carrie was quite ill with tonsillitis, and Mary Brinton was very unwell and weak. They refused to give us two of the cabins engaged, the man confessing that he had sold them over again, and would be ruined unless we gave them up. He went down on his knees and tried to shed tears, which made us more and more disgusted, as I had told him two of our party were ill. I called on Clarence Dolan to help us, and he shouted to his wife, "Rosalie, come and curse this man in French for me." Also we could not get one mouthful to eat, although it was four or five hours till dinner, and we had had nothing to eat since having breakfast in Cairo. Eckley offered to give the steward a guinea apiece for a boiled egg and a pot of hot water with which to make our own tea, but was refused. So he and I went on shore and bought from a Greek restaurant some huge sandwiches of bread and

9. Eck's adventure to the Second Cataract included a visit to Abu Seir. "The second Cataract is little inferior in scenic beauty to the First Cataract at Assuan. It lies at the north end of the gorge . . . through which the river descends in a series of rapids, over rocks of greywacke, greenstone, and granite, forming numerous islands in its course. The best point of view is the abrupt rocky hill of Abusir on the west bank. At the foot of the hill, contrasting strongly with the green of the tamarisk trees, lies a chaos of glistening black boulders, through which the river forces its way in foaming cataracts" (Karl Baedeker, *Egypt and the Sudan* [Leipzig: Karl Baedeker, 1908], 403).

beef. The Russian dinner that night was very good, and there were rows of glass carafes on the table, containing vodka with which some of us scalded our throats, thinking it was water.

It was a beautiful sight as we approached the Pireas, seeing the remains of temples on the shores, and in the distance, the Acropolis at Athens.[10] On deck at the prow, there stood a Greek merchant, who had been on the Nile with us. He had lived many years in London, and was bringing his family for the first time to see his native land; a stalwart son belonging to an English rifle regiment, and just back from India, and two daughters named Faith and Zoë, and a wife who told us she was born in Turkey, but was not a turkey!

Our stay in Athens was most interesting, and the marble-corridored hotel very delightful. One morning we were told that there was a strike among all the cab-drivers; and as several of us were not able to walk all the way to the Acropolis and up its steep flight of steps, Eckley came in beaming, and said he had got a countryman's cart to take us. This was a high, painted vehicle without springs, and the driver, who wore a velvet jacket and a gay hat, placed boards across the top of the cart. He climbed in by means of a ladder, while everybody in the hotel stared at us, and threatening looking cab-drivers stood and scowled. We jolted along the broad streets, all the guests of the cafés coming out to stare at us and grin. Eckley was delighted in having outwitted the strikers. That afternoon a number of guests at our hotel followed his example. And the next day we heard that the Crown Prince had promised the men to adjust their grievance and abolish the strike.

10. Lizzie and her party were traveling aboard a Russian steamer in the Aegean and approaching Greece and Athens through the Piraeus, the seaport of Athens. "One ought most infallibly to be early on deck, for the rugged rocky shores of the Peloponnesus are close at hand on the left, indented here and there by deep inlets or gulfs, and looking as most travelers seem to think Greece ought to look. . . . Perhaps the most trying experience to the newcomer is this landing at the Piraeus and the labor involved in getting ashore and up to Athens. . . . While the steamer is being warped to her position, a fleet of small boats, most of them flying the flags of hotels in Athens, eagerly swarm around and await the lowering of the landing stairs, meantime gesticulating violently to attract the attention of passengers on deck" (Philip Sanford Marden, *Greece and the Aegean Islands* [Boston: Houghton Mifflin, 1907], 38–42).

Another adventure of ours in Athens, I must say was very alarming. Eckley had been invited by the Ionides[11] to attend a picnic at which they were to entertain the Prime Minister. So we four ladies thought we would drive to the summer palace, and started off in two open Victorias.[12] The drivers were surly looking individuals who could speak no language but their own, which made it very difficult for us to give directions. We stopped at a restaurant to have tea, and while we were there, the drivers must have been indulging in something stronger. In fact we had to search for them a long time, which made our return rather late. The man who drove Carrie and me was very uproarious and rocked about on his seat, flourishing his whip in the air. He struck into a narrow wood road, which we hoped connected with the main road, and we made signs to him that we would get down and pick some beautiful anemones that were growing thickly in a meadow, and for him to go on. However, he jumped down, too, and with drunken cackles of laughter helped us to pick anemones until we got into the Victoria, and motioned him to follow the others as fast as possible. Before we got out of the wood, however, a branch touched his hat, and he rolled off the box, but recovered his seat and the reins. We became a good deal frightened by this time, as it began to grow dusk and not a human being in sight. In the very far distance the Acropolis was out-lined against a stormy sky, and we were going in another direction in spite of our entreaties and commands. Presently we drove through the most alarming looking little village, with only a few brigand like looking men and many huge empty wine casks rolling about the streets. Soon after this, however, and very suddenly we saw the civilized gleam of telegraph poles and heard the welcome tinkle of trolleys on a broad road leading into Athens, and shortly afterward arrived there safely. I shall always think of different colored papering in connection with that drive, as Carrie tried to divert my thoughts by planning decorations for Windy Hill.[13]

11. The Ionides are unidentifiable friends of Eck's, but this possibly refers to members of a Greek merchant family such as Constantine Ionides (1833–1900), who served as Greek consul-general in London from 1884 to 1894.

12. A Victoria is a type of open horse-drawn carriage.

13. Lizzie and Eck were in the process of building the house at Windy Hill, with approximately forty-five rooms in Drifton, Pennsylvania, which is about one hundred miles northwest of Philadelphia.

One day we walked into the great wide open gates of the King's palace, but soon saw that the frilly-skirted little sentinels on the terrace were scowling angrily at us.[14] We prepared to turn with as much dignity as possible, when a tall man in hunting clothes, and followed by dogs, went up the steps and was saluted by all eight sentinels. He took off his cap to us, and sent a fat old German butler running to say, "Der Konig hoped that die Damen would do him the honor of walking in his garden," all of which we enjoyed immensely.[15]

The pleasantest thing in Greece was our excursion to Olympia (although our drive to Eleusis was also charming) by the way of Salamis. We sat on the great marble steps of the temple of Diana, while the bees from Hymethis buzzed on the wild thyme and other enchanting flowers.[16]

I remember too, how interesting our visit was to a school for little Greek children taught by a very fine American woman. The girls stitched fine linen bands and the boys made beautiful cross-stitch samplers. They gave us each one, and then sang the Twenty Third Psalm in modern Greek. When we left, we gave the teacher enough money to buy each child a small piece of lamb to take home at Easter. We went to Olympus by rail

14. Lizzie and Carrie's impromptu meeting with the king gave them a taste of Greek politics. "The palace of the king is far less attractive, being a huge barn-like structure in the centre of the city, relieved from utter barrenness only by a very good classic portico. But nothing could be lovelier than the deep dells of the palace gardens with its jungle of flowers, shrubs, and magnificent trees. . . . Most picturesque of all are the king's body-guard, with their magnificent physique and national dress. They are big, erect fellows, clad in the short fustanella skirts of the ancient regime, the tight-fitting leggings, the pomponed shoes, the dark overjacket and the fez" (Philip Sanford Marden, *Greece and the Aegean Islands* [Boston: Houghton Mifflin, 1907], 70–71).

15. The king was George I, son of King Christian IX of Denmark. He was assassinated in 1913 (Bertold Spuler, *Rulers and Governments of the World, Vol. 2, 1492–1929* [London: Bowker, 1977], 261).

16. Lizzie and her party reached Mount Olympus via train. The games at Olympia were celebrated during a period of about one thousand years. They recurred at four-year intervals and were held in midsummer. Runners, wrestlers, discus throwers, chariot drivers, boxers, and the best from all Greece came here for the games. The ruins are dominated by the two great temples to Hera and to Zeus. The statue of Hermes by Praxiteles is housed in a small museum on the site (ibid., 262–69).

in the care of a very funny old dragoman, and the worst of it was, we could hardly understand each other at all. The chief thing he carried, besides a very imposing scimitar, was an enormous demi-john, which we feared contained the horrid mastic wine of the country. When we got to the station at Olympus, there was a tiny donkey waiting for us, and high up on the hills a very showy, temple-like building which was the new hotel, so we ladies supposed we were to take turns riding up on the donkey. On the contrary, all our luggage including the huge demi-john was piled on the poor little beast, and we were left to climb up as best we could. After a rather uneatable dinner, we thought of making some tea with materials we bought, and succeeded in getting them to understand that we wanted a little milk, when everybody in the hotel scampered out on the hillside with their short white skirts flying, and brought back a little goat which they proceeded to milk. I bought the little bell fastened to the wooden collar it wore as a memento. The next day was indeed enchanting, walking down to the old stadium, all fringed with the pale pink tamarisk and seeing the old tiled floors, the places of the high seats of honor whence the emperors and princes looked on at the races, and the pit where the statue of Hermes was found buried for concealment. Then we saw the beautiful statue itself in the little museum.

Our return to Naples and eventually Rome was an unexpected and not pleasant adventure in itself. We boarded Cook's steamer from Athens to Naples, and the trip was exquisite as we went through the Greek Isles. Our steamer arrived on time to Naples. There was the train to carry us to Rome near the wharf, and, alongside, a fine P and O steamer from Bombay. On the deck an Englishman was waving to his brother on our boat whom he had not seen for years. Well, as I put my foot on the gang-way to step off, I heard a sort of subdued hubbub, a large yellow flag was run up, the sailors took up the plank, and our steamer slowly turned around to go to the quarantine station. We were then told that the Italian doctor had found in the second cabin a man who was ill and delirious but the doctor waited until he got on shore to pronounce it cholera and to quarantine the steamer for a fortnight. The dismay was great on board and all our hopes were built on our Englishman's brother from Bombay, who shouted that he would telegraph Rome and Trieste. We anchored and a police boat circled around us to see that no one got off. At dinner a little committee of gentlemen proposed that we should raise a sum of money for the man who was ill and relieve his mind of some probable anxiety about money. A handsome Austrian countess carried around a plate which was soon filled with gold pieces, but when the committee took it down to the poor man he flung the money on the floor in scorn. After a while our English friend rowed out in speaking distance and said the best reply he could get us from Rome was that instead of being put off at the quarantine station where people generally got ill of pneumonia in dirty huts, our captain was ordered to take the steamer up the Adriatic to Trieste to be examined by Austrian doctors. I don't remember much about the two days trip except that the food became scarce, the waiters careless and that our stewardess told Carrie she was a Hungarian baroness and so poor that she gladly accepted the compassionate Carrie's gift of her own flannel wrapper! We were frightfully anxious while waiting in the harbor at Trieste until the five doctors came out to examine us, and happy indeed when they pronounced the ill man to have brain fever and not cholera. There was no train to Rome until next morning, so we spent the night in Trieste and I remember nothing about it except the delightful whipped cream they gave us hot in a copper jug with our coffee.

Lizzie's letters from this trip to Egypt and Greece add vivid details to her journal entry. Her letter of February 14 was to her younger brother, Charles St. George Sinkler, who lived at the family plantation, Belvidere, outside of Eutawville,[17] South Carolina. Lizzie called her younger brother Charlie. Lizzie mentioned how wonderful it was to receive letters from her sister-in-law, Anne, who was Anne Wickham Porcher Sinkler.[18] Lizzie referred to her two young nieces, Emily and Anne Sinkler, the daughters of Charlie and Anne. The second letter (February 21) and the third (March 1) were both to Anne.

---

17. Eutawville was a small pineland village founded by Capt. James Sinkler (1740–1800) and used as a summer residence for Charleston residents wishing to escape the heat and mosquitoes of the city. This area was also known as Old Sinklers, or Old Santee. In 1770 Captain Sinkler (Sinclair) was granted nearly six hundred acres in Craven County by George III (Dorothy Kelly MacDowell, comp., *Gaillard Genealogy: Descendants of Joachim Gaillard & Esther Paparel* [Columbia, S.C.: R. L. Bryan, 1974], 281).

18. Anne Wickham Porcher Sinkler (1860–1919).

Lizzie expressed concern for Eckley, who traveled in the midst of the Dervishes.[19] The military conditions of the Sudan in January and February of 1895 were unsettled. By the end of 1885 Mahdism controlled the Sudan. The Egyptians held only a small outpost at Suakin. The Khalifa was in control. "Gordon's head had been the first of many to be displayed in the Khalifa's new and ramshackle capital of Omdurman. . . . The frontier was fixed at Wadi Halfa. . . . One of the first British officers to be appointed to the Egyptian Army in 1883 had been Herbert Kitchener. . . . He quickly attained a reputation as the most determined and efficient officer of the new army." While Kitchener eventually defeated the Khalifa's forces at the Battle of Omdurman on September 2, 1898, the Sudan in 1895 was in the grip of the Mahdi, Mohammed Ahmed, a self-proclaimed religious leader. The Mahdi had occupied all of the Sudan, driving the Egyptians to a few encircled garrisons. The British called on Maj. Gen. Charles Gordon. He was sent to Khartum with orders to evacuate this last Egyptian and British outpost in the Sudan. The Mahdist cordon closed in, surrounding Khartum, cutting it off from the outside. On January 26, 1885, Khartum fell, and Gordon was beheaded.[20]

Pagnon's Luxor Hotel
Luxor (Upper Egypt)
Feb. 14th, 1895

Dearest Charlie,

I got such a delightful and welcome letter from you last week I think it was, but it is very hard to calculate time on the Nile. The days pass quickly, and yet it seems to me months since we have been leading this life. We are now spending a week at the Luxor Hotel,[21] as you may see from this

---

19. Dervishes are members of a Sufi Muslim mystic fraternity whose religious devotion is characterized by austere living, contemplative meditation, and whirling dancing.

20. Michael Barthorp, *War on the Nile: Britain, Egypt and the Sudan, 1882–1898* (Dorset, Eng.: Blandford Press, 1984), 133–44.

21. "There are three good hotels, but they are apt to be unpleasantly crowded during the height of the season—the months of January and February. The Luxor has accommodation for 140 guests. . . . The Luxor is luxuriously appointed and has a large garden. Electric light throughout. Billiard-room, tennis-court and steam laundry are among the up-to-date features of this hotel." The hotel also had an

extraordinary paper. I am waiting with some anxiety Eck's return from the 2nd Cataract. I got a long telegram from him last night from Wady Halfa in which he says the therm was 100 in the shade on deck and that he was going to ride a camel today on the excursion to Abou Seir. Some people who have just come back from there say they had to have an escort of 20 soldiers on camels for that trip as it is just on the frontier and the Dervishes are not to be trusted. Imagine what a fright I had last evening. Some one came in the parlor and said no one was going to the 2nd cataract next week as news had been received of fighting between the Dervishes and English troops. However it was soon found to be an old rumor of a month ago and they assured me this is the safest time to go there as the English general is up there for his annual review with 5,000 troops and a camel corps of 400. Eck was particularly bent upon this trip as there seemed to be something more unusual and adventurous about it and if the rest of us had gone all the spice would have been lacking. The steamboats are small for it, only holding 12 and there were several ladies going so it would have been too bad in me to prevent him. Excuse my dwelling on this so much but of course it occupies my mind a good deal at present.[22]

In spite of this famous climate and the cloudless blue skies we have every day the summer heat. I am suffering with neuralgia in all my teeth intensely a thing I have never had before and have had to insist on their

English doctor on the premises as well as a small church (E. A. Reynolds-Ball, *Cairo of To-Day: A Practical Guide to Cairo and its Environs* [London: Adam and Charles Black, 1899], 184–85).

22. A trip from Luxor to the second cataract was a substantial undertaking involving steam travel on the Nile to Aswan and from there to Wadi Halfa. Cook's tourist steamers provided this service into Upper Nubia. Eck's destination was Abu Simbel. "The two temples of Abu Simbel, built by Ramses II are among the most stupendous monuments of ancient Egyptian architecture. . . . The temple produces a very grand effect by moon light or at sunrise. . . . It is entirely excavated out of the solid rock. It was dedicated in the first place to Ammon-Re of Thebes and Re-Harakhte of Heliopolis, the leading deities of Egypt proper. . . . Our attention is attracted by the four colossi of Ramses II hewn out of the cliff against which their backs are placed, and arranged in pairs on each side of the entrance to the temple. Each of these figures is over 65 ft. in height" (Karl Baedeker, *Egypt and the Sudan* [Leipzig: Karl Baedeker, 1908], 395).

going to Karnak without me this morning.[23] It is certainly very strange that so many people on the boat had sore throat and colds that there were many grim jokes about this unequalled climate. I suppose it is the great changes of temperature. I have never felt such intense heat as we have had during the last week in the middle of the day, the therm frequently being 90 to 95 for hours and then delicious cool breezes and always cool enough for a blanket at night which would be very pleasant if it did not have these disastrous results.

It is very picturesque and pleasant here. This hotel is Eastern in effect with every European comfort. It is near the river but surrounded by a large garden and grove of palms besides beautiful flowering trees under which are the roses and other flowers which they irrigate every evening through numerous little trenches as no rain ever falls.[24] There is a long walk

23. The Temple of Karnak was quite near Luxor. "The walls of the various temples that form the Karnak complex produced a rich harvest of heads: here were the enemies of Egypt at the height of her empire—Hittites, Syrians, Libyans, Nubians mown down by Pharaoh's chariot or held by the hair in one improbably bunch to be dispatched with his scimitar" (Margaret S. Drower, *Flinders Petrie: A Life in Archaeology* [London: Victor Gollancz, 1985], 118). The immense Karnak complex centers on the Temple of Amun and includes courts, halls, and the imposing granite statue of Rameses II in front of the entrance to the Great Hypostyle Hall. The temple complex lay buried under sand for more than one thousand years before excavation began in the mid–nineteenth century (*Egypt Eyewitness Travel Guide* [London: Dorling Kindersley, 2001], 184). "The route from Luxor to Karnak lies straight as the crow flies across the plain, along a magnificent avenue nearly two miles long, which was once bordered with sphinxes from one end to the other. . . . That the visitor should be almost stupefied by the vastness of scale is scarcely surprising when we consider that four Notre Dame Cathedrals could be built in the outer walls of the Great Temple and that the propylon (entrance gateway) equals in breadth along the length of the nave of many English cathedrals" (E. A. Reynolds-Ball, *Cairo of To-Day: A Practical Guide to Cairo and its Environs* [London: Adam and Charles Black, 1899], 189).

24. The beauty of ancient Thebes, as Luxor was known, is noted by a contemporary guidebook: "On each side of the Nile stretches a wide belt of fertile land bounded both on the e. and w. by ranges of hills, overtopped by finely shaped peaks. . . . The verdant crops and palms which everywhere cheer the traveler as soon as he has quitted the desert, the splendid hues that tinge the valley every morning and evening, the brilliant, unclouded sunshine that bathes every object even in the winter-season, lend to the site of ancient Thebes the appearance of a wonderland,

bordered with opopanax trees which meet over head. In the house are open halls and stone flagged corridors with divans, etc. and innumerable Arab servants clad in long white nightshirts with a red sash bound round the waist and yards of white turban wound round the head. They are very neat and noiseless and do everything for you. The only woman is the English housekeeper. Outside the gates wait numbers of donkey boys with pretty white donkeys with red trappings and bead necklaces, but you hire saddles from the hotel. The horses here are very handsome and many men ride.

Yesterday afternoon we went to the races of which I enclose you a program. They were all very funny except the horse races which were most exciting. The Arab boys were riding fast Arab horses bare back. Of course the races are got up by the English. An Englishman, who I had noticed last week as being a judge or starter came up to me the day we arrived here to stay, electrified me by saying, "would you ah be good enough to run in the animal race?" "What, I said? Do you mean I will ride a buffalo or camel?" "Ah no, you might you know run a pig or a turkey, you've only got to hold the string slack!" And we found yesterday there really was a race in which about a dozen people held by strings various animals, a goat, a turkey, a beautiful little antelope, a rooster, etc., and tried to make them run. I have always heard that the English are thoroughly simple minded about their games, but I never imagined such a sight as the chaplain carefully running a turkey![25]

---

richly endowed with the gifts of never failing fertility" (Karl Baedeker, *Egypt and the Sudan* [Leipzig: Karl Baedeker, 1908], 249).

25. The Egypt that Lizzie, Carrie, and Eck were visiting had a tremendous social life from January to April. "Visitors may be roughly divided into three categories —sight-seers and tourists; winter residents and smart people, and invalids.... The winter residents, along with the official community—English officers of the Egyptian army and the army of occupation, Government officials and their families— form the Anglo-American Colony.... Cairo rather resembles Nice or Monte Carlo. ... From January to April there is an incessant round of receptions, dinner parties, balls, picnics, gymkhanas, theatricals, tennis parties and other social functions. ... When the alternative to a bicycle-gymkhana, a polo match at the Turf Club, or a lawn-tennis tournament at the Ghezireh Palace is a visit to a 'gloomy old temple,' it is only natural with young people that the ancient monuments should go" (E. A. Reynolds-Ball, *Cairo of To-Day: A Practical Guide to Cairo and its Environs* [London: Adam and Charles Black, 1899], 40–42).

The garden at Windy Hill, Drifton, Pennsylvania, 1999. Photograph by Anne LeClercq

A Scene from Algiers, *by E. A. Coxe, 1893*

Naples

The sun is warm the sky is clear
The waves are dancing fast + bright
Blue isles + snowy mountains wear
The purple noons transparent light
The breath of the moist air is light
Round its unexpanded buds
Like many a voice of one delight
The winds, the birds, the ocean-floods
The city voice itself is soft like Solitudes

I see the deeps untrammeled floor
With green + purple sea weed strown
I see the waves upon the shore
Like light dissolved in star showers thrown
I sit upon the sands alone
The light wind of the noontide
Is flashing round me
and a tone
rises from its measured motion
How sweet! did any
heart now share in
my emotion

Yet now despair itself
is mild
even as the wind + waves are
I could lie down like
a tired child
And weep away the
life of care
Which I have borne
+ still must bear
Till death like sleep
might steal on me
And I might feel in the
warm air
my cheek grow cold
and hear the sea
Breathe o'er my dying brain
Its last monotony
P.B. Shelley

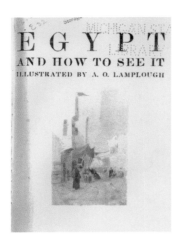

*Illustrations by A. O. Lamplough
for this publication, 1899*

Musée de l'Opéra de Vichy

Brève histoire d'un grand théâtre

Décor pour Aïda de Verdi, première œuvre représentée dans le nouvel Opéra, le 2 juin 1901.

Partition de l'Opéra de Richard Strauss, Salomé.

The theater at Vichy, 1902

The Bay of Naples, by E. A. Coxe, 1905

Scenes
from
Istanbul,
*by Warwick
Goble, 1906*

Venice

She looks a sea Cybele, fresh from Ocean
Rising with her tiara of proud towers, at air distant
With proud motion.
A Ruler of the waters and their powers
And such she was; her daughters had their dow.
From spoils of nations and the exhaustless East
Pour'd in her lap all gems in sparkling shower
In purple was she robed and of her feast
Monarchs partook + deemed their
dignity increased

Byron

Venice, *by E. A. Coxe, 1910*

Last night we were too delighted at getting a batch of letters from Cairo. Carrie got a long one from Anne who does write the nicest and most graphic letters. Carrie's perfectly devoted to her and her eyes overflowed with tears as she read her account of things at Belvidere. I never realized till now her intense devotion to everything there and am sure you have no idea of it. Her tender feeling toward you all too is very touching. We are delighted with Emily's letters. That energy of expression is very characteristic. We can't help feel worried though about Darling little Anne. I hope you are giving her cod liver oil and every thing strengthening.

Your devoted Lizzie

> Rameses
> Abydos on the Nile
> Feb. 21st, 1895
> Pagnon's Luxor Hotel

Dearest Anne,

It is seldom that I can find a day to write to you when Carrie had not just sent you a letter. But she and Eck have gone on a day's excursion and I have a nice idle time to write, so will risk repeating things. Neither Carrie nor I felt very well last night and I decided not to take the trip today, as it is 2 hours to Abydos[26] and 2 back on donkeys. This morning we found a magnificent cool day like October after the intense August-like heat at

---

26. "One of the prize locations in Egypt was Abydos, a center of the Osiris cult and a place of ancient pilgrimage. The cemeteries of Abydos had a range of thousands of years." A Frenchman, Abbé Amèlineau, "in 1894 received the concession to excavate the cemetery of the earliest kings of Egypt at Abydos. . . . Finally in 1900 [Flinders Petrie] was permitted to investigate the cemetery. Not only did he map and record and photograph what had previously been studied in a superficial way; he picked up the broken materials discarded by Amèlineau, published them, and made sense of them" (John A. Wilson, *Signs & Wonders upon Pharaoh: A History of American Egyptology* [Chicago: University of Chicago Press, 1964], 94–95). While Lizzie stayed on board, Carrie and Eck had the pleasure of a donkey ride across the plain to the Abydos. "The chief monument to be seen is the Temple of Seti I, (father of Rameses the Great) with its magnificent mural decorations and bas-reliefs. . . . On one of the walls is the famous Stela, known as the Tablet of Abydos, a piece of petrified history of the greatest value to Egyptologists. It gives a list, with date of accession, of the first seventy-seven sovereigns of Egypt" (E. A. Reynolds-Ball, *Cairo of To-Day: A Practical Guide to Cairo and its Environs* [London:

Luxor. The broad Nile was sparkling like silver and the huge white sailed boats were skimming under a fresh breeze. The great palm groves were rustling under the blue sky, and Libyan hills pink and dreaming in the distance.

Carrie began to feel she must go. She loves the excursions and takes the deepest interest in the sights. So I engaged a chair for her to be carried by 4 stalwart sailors. But at the last moment she could not stand the idea of a chair and went gaily off on a white donkey with an amulet around its neck. Eck went trolling ahead on a still smaller one with his donkey boy carrying his camera and a magnesium wire lamp to light up the tombs. They are to have lunch in the temple at Abydos and I believe it is very beautiful.

I don't regret anything however for it is too delicious on deck in this exquisite cool air and the place is the prettiest I have seen. We are lying by a green bank with a magnificent grove of palms above, and a strip of fields thick with pink poppies. On the other side of the boat is a long strip of golden sand in the middle of the river covered with pelicans and white cranes and then the great river-boats and mountains all glorified by the lovely light.

It was nice at Luxor except that the heat was very great. I suppose I got a shock of perspiration and suffered much with neuralgia in the teeth and then we were frightened about Mary Brinton who was quite ill and in bed

---

Adam and Charles Black, 1899], 181). Here is a further description: "On the right wall is the famous List of Kings. Sethos I with the censer, and the crown-prince Ramses (with the side-lock of youth) reciting hymns from a papyrus-roll, are seen revering their royal ancestors, the names of 76 of whom are inscribed in the two upper rows. The list begins with Menes, the first king of Egypt, and extends down to Sethos. . . . Above the list is the inscription: 'the performance of the prayer for the dead—may Ptah-Seker-Osiris, lord of the tomb, who dwells in the temple of Sethos, increase the gifts for the kings of Upper and Lower Egypt—by King Sethos'" (Karl Baedeker, *Egypt and the Sudan* [Leipzig: Karl Baedeker, 1908], 236–37). Abydos was an important religious center for Osiris and the cult of resurrection. Egyptians made pilgrimages and built cemeteries there. There were ritual enactments of the death and resurrection of the god, which attracted pilgrims from all over Egypt. The temples of Sethos I and Rameses II have magnificent reliefs (John Baines and Jaromir Malek, *Atlas of Ancient Egypt* [New York: Facts on File, 1980], 114–17).

several days.[27] She was worried poor soul for fear of being ill on our hands. Fortunately she was better and able to leave yesterday. We found we could get better accommodations by dividing our party so she and Becky and the maid are on an extra boat which will get to Cairo sooner as they don't stop for this excursion.

You can imagine my delight at getting Eck back safe and as brown as an Arab and my pride at hearing such good accounts of him from his fellow travelers up the Nile. They all say he was the most thorough and spirited of the party. They had a military escort of 16 men on camels to go to Abou Seir and Eck rode the camel and carried the musket of one of the soldiers for 16 miles and the men rode a donkey. As the heat was at least 100 I am too pleased he stood it so well. He got up at 3 in the morning to see the . . . [this letter ends here].

Shepheard's Hotel, Cairo,[28]

March 1st, 1895

Dearest Anne,

Although I love to write to you at all times, one sometimes feels discouraged at the thought that we are really too far apart for a regular answering

---

27. Throughout this trip Lizzie complained of neuralgia. However, Egypt from November to April was considered a likely cure for every type of ailment due to the warm climate and the low humidity. "Phthisis . . . asthma, chronic bronchitis, Bright's disease, rheumatoid arthritis, gout, insomnia, dyspepsia, and mental strain are some of the most important ailments that are at least alleviated by a visit to Egypt. . . . At both Mena House and Helwan the prevailing winds and the amount of rain are probably much the same as in Cairo. The purity of the air at both places is marked. The medical and sanitary arrangements are excellent; and there is a resident nurse under the orders of the physician who resides there" (Karl Baedeker, *Egypt and the Sudan* [Leipzig: Karl Baedeker, 1908], xxi).

28. "The leading hotels in Cairo, headed by the historical Shepheard's . . . can certainly compare favourably with the best hotels of the most fashionable Riviera watering-places. . . . The new Shepheard's, completely rebuilt in 1891, has the high reputation for comfort in the form of electric lights, lifts, telephones. . . . Shepheard's is par excellence the American hotel. . . . To visitors of a retiring disposition what are usually thought the great charms of Shepheard's, its central situation, its life and gaiety—for afternoon tea on the terrace is quite an institution of Cairo society—are regarded rather as drawbacks. In the old days there were no doubt

interchange of letters. If you could see how eagerly welcomed your letters are by us you would be pleased. You put the every day occurrences in such a vivid and cheerful light that it is delightful. Although there is so much ahead of us still and so many delightful places to see we feel that we are now on the homeward track, having been to the farthest point, particularly as we have given up Constantinople on account of the quarantine. I am amused to find that Carrie now longs to go there and is going to try to get us there if possible. I am rather glad however in some ways not to have that extra travelling and sightseeing. It will rush us less in Italy and my brain sometimes feels overtaxed with so many interesting and wonderful places. We have just got letters of Feb. 10 and 12th, full of the intense cold and heavy snow storms. It seems queer here with July heat. In fact, I quite long for a cold place and to hear a good shower of rain falling.

Yesterday there was a sort of sirocco blowing with whirlwinds of dust and sand. Carrie and I went out in a Victoria to see some old mosques and Coptic Churches after lunch and the air was like that of a furnace.[29] So this morning we made the effort to have an early breakfast and take a donkey ride before the ½ past 10 Friday service we wanted to go to. It was cooler and delightful. Donkeys are such a pleasant and easy way of getting about. You only have to put on an old dress and shade hat. Your donkey ambles along where it would be unpleasant to walk and in a crowded street or

---

compensations in the moving panorama of Oriental life which this crowded thoroughfare presented, a kaleidoscopic procession of Bedouin Arabs from the desert, camels, tattooed negroes, Turks, jeweled pashas ambling past on richly caparisoned mules, mysterious veiled figures, and other fascinating aspects of Eastern life. ... Now, instead of these picturesque motley crowds, the modern lounger on the famous terraces looks down upon a yelling crowd of donkey-boys, guides, porters, interpreters, dragomans, itinerant dealers in sham antiques and all the noisy rabble that live on the traveling Briton" (E. A. Reynolds-Ball, *Cairo of To-Day: A Practical Guide to Cairo and its Environs* [London: Adam and Charles Black, 1899], 46–47).

29. There were several ways to get around in Cairo—donkeys as well as cabs. "Generally good victorias, with two horses, are always abundant in the European quarters, and others frequented by strangers. Closed cabs (landaus) are usually to be obtained only on special order and at higher fares. ... Fares should never be paid until the end of the drive, and the passengers should give no attention to the complaints of the cabman" (Karl Baedeker, *Egypt and the Sudan* [Leipzig: Karl Baedeker, 1908], 34).

bazaar your donkey boy puts one hand at your waist and the other at the donkey's neck and shoves you along anywhere. He keeps off beggars if they become too numerous and bargains for you in the bazaars. We are getting quite accustomed to all the queer sights here: pushing up to the wall out of the way of a long string of camels loaded with immense bales of green clover so that they are half hidden, or of sugar cane.

Later: this afternoon we drove out to see the ostrich farm in the desert which was most interesting. I thought much of how you would have enjoyed it. We saw them from one day old up to ten years. They are about as big as a large hen when a day old, and the old ones look almost as big as a camel. They look too funny with their perfectly bare pink legs and thighs and huge wings of black and white plumes which they flap up and down. We saw a female sitting on eggs in a huge nest of sand and the male standing near. He relieves her every 8 or 9 hours.[30]

We drove back into Cairo just as the sun went down in a splendid golden glory, and as the evening gun was fired from the Citadel.[31] There was a sort of subdued roar from the streets and the grave Mohammedan sitting cross-legged in front of their shops and cafes lit their cigarettes and long pipes. The thirsty donkey boys seized the water pipes and began to sneak sugar cane, and from every little cook shop you smelt the frying and cooking.[32] The fast of Ramadan began on Monday and from 3 o'clock in the night

30. Lizzie and Carrie must have yearned for a bit of rural touring. A contemporary travel book recommends omitting the ostrich farm from one's itinerary if one has only a short time to stay in Cairo (E. A. Reynolds-Ball, *Cairo of To-Day: A Practical Guide to Cairo and its Environs* [London: Adam and Charles Black, 1899], 116).

31. The evening view of Cairo from the Citadel was justifiably famous. The Citadel was a fortress begun in 1176 by Saladin (Salah el-Din). Within its walls are some of the most famous sites of Cairo—the Alabaster Mosque, completed in 1857 by Said Pasha, Joseph's Well, a shaft of vast proportions dating to the ancient Egyptians, and the wonderful view. "The prospect from the southern ramparts is justly famous and may be included among the world's most famous points of view. The Citadel is worth visiting at sunset for the view alone" (ibid., 86–91).

32. Lizzie and Carrie were rubbing shoulders with native life in the bazaars. "Native manners and customs can be well observed in the region of the bazaars. . . . One seems to meet here every costume of Europe, Asia, and Africa; and the kaleidoscopic varieties of brilliant and fantastic colouring are bewildering to a

until sunset no Mohammedan can eat, drink or smoke.[33] Some of them become very savage and fanatical in this month and the French papers here are publishing the most outrageous things about the tyranny of the English and the danger of the Egyptians rebelling and having a great massacre of Europeans during Ramadan. I don't mind telling you, as by the time you get this we will either be massacred or safe out of Egypt.

Cairo is extremely gay and crowded and it is quite dazzling even to see the ball dresses at dinner. Eck went to a fancy ball at the Gesirah palace.[34] He had his dress coat lined with blue satin and his hair powdered and that

----

stranger. Solemn and impassive looking Turks, gently ambling past on gaily-caparisoned mules, grinning negroes from the Soudan, melancholy looking Fellahs in their scanty blue kaftans, cunning featured Levantines, green turbaned Shereefs, and picturesque Bedouins from the dessert make up the mass of this restless throng" (E. A. Reynolds-Ball, *Cairo of To-Day: A Practical Guide to Cairo and its Environs* [London: Adam and Charles Black, 1899], 74–75).

33. "During the fast of the month Ramadan, from daybreak to sunset eating and drinking are absolutely prohibited, and the devout even scrupulously avoid swallowing their saliva. . . . Many shops and offices are entirely closed during this month. As the Arabic year is lunar, and therefore eleven days shorter than ours, the fast of Ramadan runs through all the seasons in the course of thirty-three years" (Karl Baedeker, *Egypt and the Sudan* [Leipzig: Karl Baedeker, 1908], lxvi).

34. This was probably the Ghezireh Palace, on the left bank of the Nile. The Khedive in 1882 had many private palaces including Abdeen, Kasr-en-Nil, and Ghezireh. Each had beautiful gardens (J. A. McCoan, *Egypt* [New York: Peter Fenelon Collier, 1898], 51). The fact that Eck was invited to a fancy-dress ball was not at all unusual for the time. "The official balls and receptions at the Khedivial Palace demand more than an incidental notice. . . . The invitations to the Khedivial ball are usually sent to foreign visitors through their minister or consul, and as everybody spending the winter at Cairo looks upon a ticket almost as a right, there is sometimes a certain amount of friction between the accredited representatives of the different powers and the Kehdive's court officials. According to a well authenticated story the Khedive once returned the proposed list of guests sent him by the United States Consul General, with an observation that only those of noble birth were eligible. The Consul promptly replied that 'Every American citizen considered himself a king in his own right.' This brought the autocratic sovereign to his bearings, and not only was the list passed, but it is said that invitations were sent besides to all the guests at Shepheard's en bloc!" (E. A. Reynolds-Ball, *Cairo of To-Day: A Practical Guide to Cairo and Its Environs* [London: Adam and Charles Black, 1899], 42).

made him a diplomat. He got home between 1 & 2 and at ½ past 8 in the morning had an engagement to ride out to the desert to see a review of the English troops with a Chicago girl. The Khedive was there and I hear it was a great sight. We are very glad for the Egyptians to be impressed by the English power. The Khedive looks like a sulky boy and naturally is very restless under the English control.

Oliver has really been very sick for several days, but is now better and up. I was very much worried about him as the Dr. was very grave about him. Mary Brinton has recovered from her attack at Luxor. Carrie looks well and fat and I am well and (I hope) thin. Speaking of thin, they say Aleck Coxe has lost 100 lbs. since his illness but does not look thin. I hope you have got 2 or 3 letters I wrote you and one to Charlie on the Nile. With my dear love to you all I am your devoted Lizzie.

Following is a letter fragment that comes at the end of this trip. The party is now in the Memphis area, and left for Alexandria and the steamer to Naples. Lizzie has her stationery from Shepheard's Hotel, but is in fact moored on the Nile River enjoying the relaxation of one of Cook's Nile steamers. The letter describes a trip by donkey to the burial site of Saqqara, where over fifteen royal pyramids have been found, including the step pyramid of Netjerykhet Djoser and the pyramid of Wenis, the last king of the Fifth Dynasty. The site is over six kilometers long.[35]

Shepheard's Hotel, Cairo, 1895

Shepheard's Cairo

This is covered with large beautiful Persian rugs and there is a piano, tables, many comfortable chairs of every kind where one sits and talks. Afternoon tea is served here and delicious Turkish coffee after meals. There is a writing room also on this deck and the dining saloon. The meals are excellent, as good as Shepheards and during lunch Al Raschid, our head Dragoman walks up and down announcing any program for the afternoon and telling us about the places we are passing. He is a very handsome Arab and has different gorgeous suits all of silk and wears a beautiful turban wound round his Fez. We have not taken the trouble yet to make many

35. John Baines and Jaromir Malek, *Atlas of Ancient Egypt* (New York: Facts on File, 1980), 142–51.

acquaintances but the passengers seem a nice set and of varied national-ities. We came on board at 10 yesterday morning and our friends the Har-risons, who made the trip up the Nile before we came, came to see us off bringing Carrie flowers. Mr. Harrison gave Eck the leggings off his own legs. He introduced us to all the officials and stewards in such terms that I am sure they expect very "big baksheesh."

When we got to Saqqara after lunch there was an immense throng of donkeys and Arabs waiting and Raschid selected the best, beat the oth-ers away with his kourbash and lifted us on. He had a white donkey for me with a red saddle and necklaces of cowie beads around its neck. He said his "best lady" had to have 2 donkey boys. They wear one garment, a long blue cotton skirt belted round the waist and in the baggy part above seem to carry all sorts of things. Mine produced oranges from it when I got thirsty. Carrie's put her cloth jacket with his to carry, and Eck's brought out from his a human skull of a mummy and begged him to buy it. Fancy this pro-cession winding along a narrow path through beautiful palm groves, boundless green fields of sweet smelling grasses, beans and young sugar cane and blue flax and then Bedouin villages where children run after you yelling baksheesh and the prettiest little girls offer to sell you their beads and brass ear rings.[36]

As we went through a narrow street a girl came out of one of the mud huts and laughing mischievously placed her brown naked baby on my lap to my great fright. At last we came to the red sand of the desert and the pyramids and tombs of Saqqara rising up on all sides against the blue sky. Such a blue, blue sky. Under these sands are buried great sphinxes and stat-ues excavated years ago, but as they were too heavy to remove the sands have covered them again. Besides the pyramids containing sarcophagi of

---

36. Lizzie noted that Egyptians of all ages expected *baksheesh*. "The average Ori-ental regards the European traveler as a Croesus, and sometimes too as a mad-man,—so unintelligible to him are the objects and pleasures of traveling. He therefore looks upon him as fair game, and feels justified in pressing upon him with a perpetual demand for bakshish, which simply means 'a gift.' Travellers are often tempted to give for the sake of affording temporary pleasure at a trifling cost, forgetting that the seeds of insatiable cupidity are thereby sown, to the infinite annoyance of their successors. . . . Bakshish should never be given except for ser-vices rendered, or to the aged and crippled" (Karl Baedeker, *Egypt and the Sudan* [Leipzig: Karl Baedeker, 1908], xxiii).

kings and the tombs of rich men, they say the ancient tombs of the poor occupy about 20 miles under these sands and you see bones, pottery and scraps of mummy cloth everywhere. We dismounted and went into a famous tomb of Ti, a man of great property apparently. There were several chambers. The walls covered with spirited scenes describing his life and the work going on, on his estates.[37]

37. The tomb of Ti was excavated by the famous French Egyptologist Mariette, who was from 1858 to 1881 director of the official excavations in Egypt. Ti was the royal architect and manager of the pyramids of King Neferirkare. The tomb originally stood above ground but during the eons was buried by sand. The mural reliefs still retain their original color and give a dramatic view of everyday life in ancient Egypt. The range of scenes is vast: cooking poultry, fattening geese, feeding cranes, sailing a ship, winnowing corn, reaping, shaping a tree trunk in the process of building a ship, carpenters making a door, an estate office, cattle feeding, plowing, tilling, sowing, rams treading on seed, cattle driven trough a river, dwarfs leading dogs, peasant women with offerings, and the great Ti sailing through the marshes (ibid., 145–55).

CHAPTER FOUR

France, "In Our Own Car," 1902

Lizzie and Eckley took many trips to France and Switzerland. On this journey to France, Lizzie was accompanied by her brother Wharton Sinkler, whom she affectionately called Bud, and his wife, Ella Brock Sinkler. The group also included Lizzie's nieces Emily Wharton Sinkler and Elizabeth Allen Sinkler Stevens. Lizzie included the nieces for the ostensible purpose of showing them the world and broadening their horizons. In truth, she was teaching values, literature, poetry, and art throughout all these expeditions. She was anxious that her extended family not languish in a Southern, provincial backwash. She gave each girl a diary to record the experiences and sights. One of these diaries survived and was authored by Elizabeth Stevens, dated 1902. It is cited here for amplification.

French roads were excellent even in horse and buggy days. France had the best road system on the Continent. Still there were problems with dust and dirt. Not until 1913 did the French started to put down asphalt highways. Michelin introduced the modern automobile tire in 1895, at which date the Automobile Club de France was formed. The Riviera and the area around Paris received the first modern roads. However, the French had greatly improved all their roads for cycling even before the first Peugeots and Citroens. The touring party of Lizzie, Eck, Wharton, Em, and Liz must have been a curious sight with top down, scarves flying, and brass candelabra for dining al fresco. Following is Lizzie's journal entry.

> No one can imagine until they have tried it, the delight of travelling in
> Europe in one's own car. From the moment when you see the gigantic
> box containing the precious thing swung on shore, it is a perpetual plea
> sure, and most of all interesting to see it dangling in the air like a huge
> beetle when they put it off at Boulogne. That day we ran all the way to

Amiens after lunch—Bud's first experience of French roads, and keep to the left instead of the right. Quite by chance we went to the same hotel where over twenty years ago we stayed and Mary made her famous exclamation, "Oh, look at the stork and its young," for as I looked out of the rather shabby little window into the courtyard, there was a gigantic stork strutting around the fountain, and at its heels a rusty old black raven! I see in my mind's eye lovely visions of walking around the Cathedral in the moonlight, and of Beauvais and other enchanting places where we stopped next day. After our visit to Paris we began our unexplored journey down to Avignon.[1] We determined to discover all we could for ourselves, and ran along the broad, smooth roads bordered with trees and fields scarlet with poppies through little villages until we got hungry and came to one where the little inn on the street had very white window curtains and big tubs of very pink oleanders on the flag stones outside, and then we went in, and in spite of the blue smocked farmers sitting at their lunch, the land lady quickly prepared us a delightful meal.

On we went, spending nights at Orleans and Bourges, which was a charming place to stop at. The deep roof over the hotel door was completely covered with yellow roses, and nearby was the old Archbishop's garden laid out by Le Notre and full of yew hedges and roses, and then

1. While Lizzie gives short shrift to Paris, her niece Elizabeth Sinkler Stevens records the experience with keen delight: "On Wednesday the 9th we spent the whole day traveling and at 6 o'clock in the evening Paris with all its splendor burst upon us! We felt too overwhelmed with joy and excitement when we saw this lovely city. I have never imagined anything so fascinating and charming as it is. . . . On Thursday 10th Eck took Em and me for a lovely drive ending up by going to see Napoleon's Tomb. . . . Saturday afternoon we took such a very nice drive up the lovely Champs Elysee and through the Bois de Boulogne. The latter is too beautiful being like a very thick green forest with fine roads running through it. There are a great many fashionable open air cafes in it the finest being the Cascade. It was too amusing to drive about and see all the fine people, mostly very much berouged and blacked up ladies drawing in solemn state in splendid carriages and pair and very often accompanied only by an excruciatingly ugly tiny little dog. We took tea at the Cascade, then bought delicious waffles and drove merrily home. . . . Wednesday, 16th. We went to the dressmaker where we tried on lovely silks that Auntie is giving Em and me. Auntie gave each of us 20 francs and we are buying some lovely pictures, most of them facsimiles of those we saw in the Louvre" (Elizabeth Sinkler Stevens, diary, 1902, in the possession of author LeClercq).

the quaint old Maison de Jacques Coeur, and the most beautiful old Cathedral where there is the black Madonna, and much beautiful windows and quaint carvings.[2] Then every morning enjoying getting back in to our home-like car, full of our own comforts, and adding flowers and baskets of fruit—even a pair of old brass candlesticks, as we went along.[3] And (there was) Eck sitting so happily with Bud, his map and guide book, and pocket full of silver, and in spite of neither of them speaking French, getting along and finding the way with very little help from me.

At last we reached Avignon, surrounded with its old walls, and the Rhone rushing outside with the curious crenelated bridge over it and the old fortified palace of the Popes rising impressively on the edge of the town.[4] As it was late in the season we got the best rooms in the hotel—

2. "We come now to the gables standing over the street. There are many and charming specimens in Bourges. The most striking mansion of all is that of Jacques Coeur, the Bourges jeweler, father of an Archbishop of this his native city. Throughout the house is introduced his canting device, a human heart and the scallop shell of S. James. His motto is also graven, 'A vaillants coeurs rien impossible.' . . . He had humour, a quaint conceit, this man of gold and jewelry. He had the very knocker to his door made to strike upon a heart. Under the eaves of his observatory he had his negro sculptured hugging his money-box, and a little beyond an angel exhibiting his newly acquired coat of arms" (S. Baring-Gould, *In Troubadour-Land: A Ramble in Provence and Languedoc* [London: W. H. Allen, 1891], 315, 316).

3. Sitting in the back seat, Elizabeth Sinkler Stevens (Liz) had a slightly different perspective on the road trip: "As we rushed along we had the entire right of way, because as soon as people saw us they would just scuttle out of our way full tilt. We noticed tho that a great many of the people looked at us very vindictively and our driver told us that the poorer French classes considered automobiles a perfect scourge as they just went tearing thru the country, often running over animals and sometimes even children, and then would dash on again before anybody could catch them. In fact we did run over and kill a goose which of course Auntie paid largely for but the innocent always suffer for the wicked and later when we were passing by a wagon, the driver of it leant out and gave Auntie a terrible crack with his whip and a bad little boy flung a big stone and hit Eck on the arm" (Elizabeth Sinkler Stevens, diary, 1902, in the possession of author LeClercq).

4. "Avignon is completely surrounded by its old walls and towers. Much of the space inside is now occupied by gardens and vineyards. . . . Above Avignon is a very large island, and below it the Durance enters the Rhone through a lacework of rubble-beds. Then immediately under the Rocher des Domes is the mighty river sweeping on with strong purpose, and half-bridged by a quaint old structure, built

a beautiful big parlour full of mirrors and gilding and tapestry, for it
had once been a palace. It had a balcony on the courtyard, and the great
branches of an unknown tree pushed up into the windows. But Eck
had the most interesting room, for they gave him the one that Napoleon
occupied when he came back from Elba and landed at Frejus. They took
the key of the room out of a glass case where it hung in the hall. From
Avignon we made excursions to Orange where there is the beautiful
Roman Arch, and to Nîmes where is the famous Maison Carre, the most
beautiful piece of architecture—now a museum—and nearby a park with
the loveliest fountains. Then we stopped at San Remy to look at the noble
monument put up by Julius Caesar in the first century to one of his gen-
erals. Then to Arles where a delightful little boy with shaggy black hair
guided us to the museum dedicated to Mistrale, the Provencal poet who
made Provence famous, and where they have kept reverently everything
connected with him from his cradle up. Then the boy showed us with
dramatic remarks the street of the Dead with the many fine old Roman
sarcophagi and the beautiful old Amphitheatre where they sometimes
have bull fights and every summer the "Theatre Francaise" sends its company to act a classic play. The little boy pointed to two handsome women
with immense bows on their heads and with supreme pride said, "Voila
Mesdames, 'les belles arlesiennes!'" Before getting to Avignon we had
spent a night at Valence, where the poor hotel was made up for by break-
fasting in the lovely garden. All this country in the south of France was
very sunbaked and dry but full of beauty—Hedges of scarlet pomegran-
ates tall rows of pointed furs to screen off the mistral and showy wild
flowers. We often met great flocks of sheep, some times their wool cut
into rosettas and ornaments like poodles. Of course, we saw near Avignon
the picturesque Pont du gard—the three storied bridge and aqueduct.
Then we spent two restful days at Vichy where the fashionable crowds
visiting the springs entertained the girls very much, and the gay Casino

---

between 1177 and 1185 under the direction of S. Benezet. . . . There were originally
seventeen arches in the bridge, resting on eighteen piers. This bridge is celebrated
with the children's song: 'Sur le Pont d'Avignon tout le monde danse, danse; Sur
le Pont d'Avignon tout le monde danse en rond'" (S. Baring-Gould, In Troubadour-
Land: A Ramble in Provence and Languedoc [London: W. H. Allen, 1891], 277).

and Parisian shops and the beautiful park where all day long people sat and read and embroidered under the lindens and plane trees while pretty string bands played. Also the comfort of the delightful and luxurious Hotel des Ambassadeurs,[5] which has now been turned into a convalescent hospital, where among others our dear friend, Tom Hirst, died of his gallant wounds.

After Vichy we crossed the Cevennes, through dark fir woods and slopes bright with the yellow almond scented bloom.

Next we stopped at Aix en Provence, where the Hotel was very plain and rustic and quaint although I enjoyed seeing a man with a green baize apron on polishing the red tiles with which each room was floored, with a thick red stuff he had a bowl full of until they looked like carnelians. The hotel was on a broad street arched over with ilex trees, and down the middle of it were huge fountains in the fashion of Bernini pouring out streams of boiling hot water, where horses patiently quenched their thirst. Next day we went on past Frejus where Napoleon landed when he returned from Elba, and over the Esterels, which were less picturesque and more alarming at close quarters, as our long car found it hard to turn round the "hair pin curves" without going over the precipices backward. Our object then was to get to San Rafael beyond Nice, which our friend, Marjoni, had told us was a fascinating place to stay. However, when we got there the beautiful white hotels and casino and villas were all closed—the promenade of palm trees and green seats above the sea deserted and the colouring was so brilliant, the sapphire blue sea and sky, the dazzling white of the Moorish pinnacles of the buildings, like iced cakes, made it all look like a wonderful chromo.

After getting a scanty meal on the porch of some sort of saloon, we flew along the great Corniche road passing many beautiful villas

5. The Grand Hotel Des Ambassadeurs & Continental is advertised as being on the park and facing the casino. Key attractions included an elevator, electric light throughout, lawn tennis, post telegraph, and adjoining telephone. "Entirely rearranged and considerably enlarged. Is the most elegant, comfortable and best situated in Vichy, and the only one frequented by the Royal Family of England. A part of the hotel is arranged and warmed especially for the winter season. It is the only hotel at Vichy having a general hygienic installation. Pension from 12 fr. per day" (R. Lambert Playfair, *Handbook for Travellers in Algeria and Tunis* [London: John Murray, 1895], index, 43).

and palaces all wrapped in an enchanted slumber—the pale green blinds closed, the high white walls covered with cascades of pink climbing geraniums and big magnolia trees covered with great blossoms. We passed Cannes, which we had known so full of life and gaiety, as quiet as the others were under the magic touch of the spell. We seemed to fly furtively along the white road as if pursued, and covered with the fine white dust like a veil. At last we found a resting place at Monte Carlo, in the famous Hotel de Paris opposite the Casino that brings trouble and despair. Everything was almost empty, but still it was exciting to see the great gambling halls. Eck gave each of us a ten franc piece to put down, and as Liz quickly began to win she stopped in terror. Emily made a few francs too, and spent them on presents for us all.

CHAPTER FIVE

Trekking to Khartum, 1905

In March of 1905 Lizzie was traveling with Eck, Carrie, and Mary Jane Brinton. Their destination was Khartum. It was only eight years after General Kitchener had subdued the Madhi and the Dervish hordes at the Battle of Omdurman on September 2, 1898. The country was under British control, and the British had inducted the children of the Khalifa into their civil service.

Lizzie's descriptive account of the trip into Upper Nubia gives new and exciting details about travel at that time by train and boat. Eckley returned in 1909 to finance a major excavation at Wadi Halfa,[1] near Buhen. The trip to Luxor was enhanced by Lizzie's excitement at seeing her two nieces: Anne Wickham Sinkler and Emily Wharton Sinkler, the daughters of Charlie and Anne Sinkler. Emily was a great flirt and had many British beaux and admirers. She had green eyes, masses of auburn curls worn atop her head, and was petite. Anne was a lovely, petite brunette with green eyes. Their excitement over a trip from the South Carolina Low Country to Egypt was captured in the enthusiasm of their arrival. Lizzie described shrieks of laughter and hugs and kisses. Lizzie's letters were to her brothers Wharton and Charlie and to her sister-in-law Anne. The journal entries

---

1. Wadi Halfa is an important archaeological site in Upper Nubia. It was near Abu Simbel and across the Nile from Eck's camp at Buhen, a town of the Old Kingdom. It had a Middle Kingdom fort and temples of Isis and Min built by Amenophis II and the Horus of Buhenbuilt by Hatshepsut, Tuthmosis III, and Taharqua. The latter two temples are now removed to Khartum. Note that both Lizzie and her contemporaries referred to "Wadi" as "Wady" (John Baines and Jaromir Malek, *Atlas of Ancient Egypt* [New York: Facts on File, 1980], 187).

plus the letters give a vivid description of this part of the world shortly after the British had made it accessible for travel. Lizzie and her party were treated to the care of a very knowing dragoman, Raschid. Lizzie noted that Raschid had accompanied the Kaiser on his famous trip to Palestine. Having a personal guide in Egypt would have given Lizzie and Eck an added sense of security.[2] Following is Lizzie's journal entry.

> Our next visit to Egypt was most interesting, for our object then was Khartoum, only six years after General Kitchener had captured it in his bloody battle of Omdurman.[3] We landed at Naples, which is always

2. "The Kaiser was out of sorts. Neither England nor Russia seemed inclined to offer him any advantages so he decided to try his hand in the Middle East. For months he had talked about a trip to Constantinople, and the Holy land, which was under Turkish rule, and on October 12, 1898, he finally set forth, accompanied by the Empress and a suite of fifty. He sailed on the *Hohenzollern* to Constantinople and spent several days as the Sultan's guest. . . . He then took ship to Haifa, from which the imperial party proceeded to Jerusalem by horse, camping each night by the roadside. Despite the splendid tents and the many servants, the heat was so overpowering, and the flies so bad, that most of the entourage regarded the pilgrimage as a severe ordeal. The Emperor, however, remained enthusiastic, and his entrance into Jerusalem on October 19th was staged as a magnificent spectacle. Mounted on a black charger, dressed in gleaming white with a gold eagle at the top of his helmet, William led his brilliantly arrayed court through the gates of the Holy City" (Virginia Cowles, *The Kaiser* [New York: Harper & Row, 1963], 164–65).

3. Beginning in June 1896, the British general Horatio Herbert Kitchener began the task of retaking the Sudan from the Khalifa and the Dervishes. He began with the construction of a railroad to transport troops and supplies for the campaign. His force was made up of British officers with Egyptian and Sudanese troops. His first destination was Dongola. After capturing that, Kitchener constructed a new rail line 225 miles across the Nubian desert from Wadi Halfa to Abu Hamed. Reinforced by British troops in January 1898, General Kitchener defeated a large Dervish army under Mahmud in April 1898 on the dusty hot desert plain of the Atbara. Kitchener now assembled a force of 8,200 British and 17,600 Egyptians and Sudanese with magazine rifles, machine-guns, and howitzers and with camels, horses, mules, and donkeys. He also had gunboats on the Nile opposite Khartum, which began pounding the mud-brick city. The Dervish forces consisted of over 65,000 men, armed with swords and spears. They attacked with force on the morning of September 2, 1898, and the slaughter was immense. The lethal power of modern weapons took their toll on the heroic massed charges of the enemy. In the end there were over 10,000 Dervishes dead (Barthorp, *War on the Nile*, 130–90).

very slow and trying, and the custom-house most disagreeable;[4] Carrie insisted that Eck and I should go on and secure our rooms at the hotel, while she and Mary Jane struggled with the custom-house. So we got into a ricketty little Victoria, a big fox-tail dangling between the horse's eyes (according to their odd custom) and were followed by a swarm of eloquent and dramatic beggars. As we approached the Grand Hotel, at the end of the Via Nazionale we began to meet streams of our fellow passengers who had been turned away. They said it was useless for us to go in as there was not a room to be had.[5] However Eck insisted that they would have kept rooms for us, as we had written for them from Philadelphia. So I sat hopelessly on my valise in the marble vestibule, while he pushed through the crowd to the desk. He returned with a very polite clerk, who was shocked that Madame had not expected them to keep the same suite she had had before. These were the lovely rooms with the exquisite view

4. Carrie, Lizzie, and Eck had landed in Naples as there were direct steamers each week from Naples to Alexandria. The trip was four nights, or sixty-six hours. The Navigazione Generale Italiana had a steamship leaving every Wednesday at three PM, reaching Alexandria on Sunday at three P.M. Egypt was a popular destination in the season (January to March), and there were regular connections from Venice, Genoa, Marseilles, Trieste, and Constantinople (Karl Baedeker, *Egypt and the Sudan* [Leipzig: Karl Baedeker, 1908], 3, 4).

5. The Grand Hotel was indeed a "very first class hotel"; it was listed as being close to the Via Nationale, costing from 61 to 131 lira, and being closed from June 15 to September 15. Lizzie and her party went to tea at Caflisch, which was listed as a tearoom on Via Chiaja. "The incomparable situation of Naples has at all times attracted strangers. The best time to visit it is April and May, or October and November. . . . Still la bella Napoli is beautiful at all seasons, and in no small degree in summer, when nature shows herself in her full splendour. Then too, life can be very pleasant there, if one adopts the habits of the natives, who spend the hot hours of the day in the cool rooms of their houses, and enjoy a long siesta in the afternoon. . . . The life of the people of Naples is very animated, and characterized by great freedom and singularity; hawkers, newspaper-sellers and beggar-boys swarm around the stranger in the most obtrusive manner; the best way to get rid of them is to take absolutely no notice of them. . . . The churches are opened early in the morning; all except the cathedral are closed for 2–3 hours in the middle of the day. . . . The museums are, as a rule, open from 10 to 4. . . . Nobody should miss visiting the Italian theatre (opera, ballet, drama, comedy, popular pieces and marionettes)" (Albert Goldschmidt, *Naples and Environs* [Berlin: A. Goldschmidt, 1913], 10, 11, 13).

of the Bay and Vesuvius. By this time Carrie arrived, and a delightful
tea was ready; and soon afterwards beautiful flowers came from a Berlin
Colonel, who had crossed with us, and brought us letters of introduction
from John Newbold. He was such a charming man, so interesting and
polished; alas! what has he done since? I hope he was too old for this war,
or died before it began!

We took a steamer from Naples to Alexandria, passing Etna and
Stromboli, and going through the beautiful straits of Messina. After reaching Cairo we went up the Nile as usual in a Cook steamer, and were glad
to find Raschad again chief dragoman.[6] Since we had seen him, he had
been in personal charge of the Kaiser on his famous trip to Palestine. He
was so delighted to see Eck, that he kissed him on both cheeks before Eck
could prevent it. We changed at Assuan to a smaller boat, which was sim-
pler but very delightful.[7] We sat all day on the open upper deck, seeing
groves of palms submerged by the great dam, waving their feathery tops
above the water. Once we saw a great arrow-shaped flock of cranes that
seemed to fill half the heavens, and once we saw an enormous water-bird
swimming across the river; this later proved to be a boy with a sheaf of
straw under each arm. After passing the first cataract the sand became a
most beautiful copper colour. It was wonderfully picturesque to see the
women in their long trailing black veils walking along the side of a hill

6. On this Nile excursion Carrie, Lizzie and Eck are on the *Rameses the Great,*
which had eighty berths and took ten days for the voyage to Aswan; there they
changed to another Cook steamship, the *Prince Abbas,* for the four-day trip to Halfa
and Upper Nubia (Karl Baedeker, *Egypt and the Sudan* [Leipzig: Karl Baedeker,
1908], 197, 373).

7. Aswan at this time was the capital of the southernmost province of Upper
Egypt. "The once considerable trade in the products of the Sudan and Abyssinia
has greatly fallen off since the Mahdist revolt. . . . The Nile here divides into several arms, separated by granite rocks and islands, the largest of which is Elephan-
tine. . . . On account of its equable and dry climate Assuan is much visited as a
winter resort. . . . The sportsman will find the neighbourhood of Assuan of great
interest, the game including wolves, jackals, foxes, hyaenas, and desert grouse." The
dam at Aswan was completed in December 1902 and was the work of English
engineers. It was constructed to dam up the water of the Nile to a height of eighty-
three feet so that a regular supply could be furnished for the irrigation of the country during time of low water—roughly April to July (ibid., 349, 365–66). Note that
Lizzie and her contemporaries spoke of Assuan, but today it is known as Aswan.

with a jar of water on their heads, and above them the brilliant blue sky. The women even ploughed with their black garments trailing while the men worked at the sakiyehs perfectly naked, like bronze statues. Once we tied up for the night at Korusko before dark. Many of the passengers walked out on the banks, and found a little garden planted by some homesick Englishman, with home flowers and herbs, among them mint, which Mr. Lathrop, a Virginian on board, brought in to make mint-juleps.[8] Mr. Lathrop was much disgusted to find that when we arrived at Wady Halfa, we intended going on to Khartoum; for, being a great traveller himself, he hated to be out-travelled. He was so alarming in his account of the dangers, that it took all my courage to go on to please Eck. As we drew up to the pier at Wady Halfa a big Nile boat with 3 decks was disembarking a regiment of Soudanese soldiers to the spirited music of the native pipes, which sound wonderfully like the Highland bag-pipes. The Soudanese are fine soldiers, and when they are in camp, the English government allows each man support for four wives!

We found the military train waiting to go on to Khartoum, and it being late in the season, and no tourists but ourselves and a fat old German counsellor with a young attendant, and two Englishmen (who got off soon in the midst of the desert to hunt) each of us, including Mary Jane, was given a large stateroom, with a hammock, a large chair, a table and an electric fan.[9] An English officer in charge of the train came around and asked if we would like to engage baths at General Kitchener's bathing station; so early next morning every one might have been seen in wrappers and carrying sponges, going to the long, low adobe building, where graceful young Arabs in white gowns and red sashes, gave us each a room with a large bath and clean towels. The days on the train passed quickly; the English Commander brought round at meals, telegraphed bulletins of

8. This is Korosko in Nubia, where the Nile makes a huge bend and there is a caravan route across the desert from Korosko to Abu Hamed.
9. "The construction of the railway to Khartum was undertaken in 1896–97 in order to support the advance of the Anglo-Egyptian army; and in spite of the enormous difficulty of laying a railway line across the sandy and stony surface of the desert, the work was so energetically carried on that it advanced almost a mile a day.... The stony desert gradually gives place to undulating sand hills.... At Abu Hamed there are baths for passengers at the railway station" (Karl Baedeker, *Egypt and the Sudan* [Leipzig: Karl Baedeker, 1908], 407).

news of the day, and Eck enjoyed talking with the men very much.
He brought up a Greek merchant who asked to be introduced to me.
He had fought in the English army as an officer at Omdurman, and
now lived there. He said it was a pity we had come so late in the season,
as the few officers' wives had gone and the Sirdar had just taken his wife
to Cairo. Eck had a letter of introduction to him, and also to Slatin Pasha,
who was likewise away.[10] The Greek warned us of the danger of the sun
and said sunstroke meant death, and we must wear helmets.[11] He also
invited us to take tea with his wife on Sunday afternoon.

After a while we came to the great bridge over the Atbara, which the
Pencoyd Iron Works built so finely, and made a great triumph of; but it
was sad to see the little graveyard near-by, where about twenty of the
workmen had paid for the glory with their lives.[12] The Blue Nile comes
in there, and one has a mysterious feeling that down its waters have been
brought treasures of ivory, gold, frankincense and myrrh. One morning
after gazing out for some time at the dreary expanse of desert, broken

10. Slatin Pasha, also known as Rudolf Anton Karl von Slatin, led a far-flung life.
He was in the Sudan in 1874 and served in Egypt under General Gordon from
1878. He was appointed governor of Darfur in 1881. He was captured by the Mah-
dis and held prisoner from 1884 to 1895. He escaped to Cairo and was made pasha
by the Khedive in 1895 and British inspector general of the Sudan from 1900 to
1914. He was the author of *Fire and Sword in the Sudan: A Personal Narrative of
Fighting and Serving the Dervishes, 1879–1895,* trans. F. R. Wingate (London:
Edward Arnold, 1896), cited in *Merriam-Webster's Biographical Dictionary,* 1995.
11. The climate in March in Upper Nubia could be exceedingly hot. "At Khartum the maximum heat is reached in April and September. Violent sand storms
are frequent from May to September, followed by deluges of rain which are apt to
cause fever. . . . Visitors to Khartum usually feel languid and indolent for the first
few days of their stay, and are apt to suffer from swollen glands" (Rudolph Carl,
Freiherr von Slatin, *Fire and Sword in the Sudan: A Personal Narrative of Fighting
and Serving the Dervishes, 1879–1895,* trans. F. R. Wingate [London: Edward
Arnold, 1898], 406).
12. "To the left of the railway is a cemetery containing graves of the British soldiers who died in the hospital of Atbara after the battle. The railway is here carried
by an iron bridge over the river Atbara, the channel of which is dry from April to
June. The battle of Atbara took place on April 8, 1898. Kitchener marched from
Berber to Hudi on the Atbara, whence he attacked the Emir Mahmud. The victory
of the English opened the way for a further advance to the Sudan" (ibid., 410).

only by a sheik's tomb, or a little group of graves, I sat reading by my
window, when someone came to the door and said, "Look at the mirage."
There, at a short distance from the train, a beautiful river was flowing
rapidly along, with a fringe of palm trees waving in the breeze, and the
water sparkling in the sunlight. I said, "Mirage indeed! When did we get
near the Nile?" For truly it was hard to believe it to be merely an illusion.
For two or three hours we gazed at this wonderful sight; sometimes the
river seemed quite far off, with little inlets and bluffs and tall trees; then
a little farther on, the stream seemed to have turned and danced along
in glittering waves almost touching the train. It was indeed a marvelous
experience.

When we reached Omdurman we had to cross the broad river to
reach Khartoum. There was a government steamboat, but we went in a
felucca, and the sailors had a delightful lilac monkey, who sat up on the
mast and made faces at us. We were greatly impressed by all that the
English had done in those six years. They had rebuilt Gordon's palace
and had founded a college where the sons of his enemies were being educated, a zoo and a garden for collecting rare specimens, and a very decent
hotel with large piazzas all around.[13] The trees and flowers on this bank
of the Nile were very beautiful, many of the mimosa kind, yellow and red,
and vines with great white flowers. They said we were blessed in having a
cool wind, and no sand storm.

While there an Irish officer named Murphy staying at the hotel took
possession of us and was most kind and attentive. He also brought us a
very smart, black, young Arab, Mahomet, who was quite invaluable, and

---

13. Khartum, the capital of the Sudan and the residence of the sirdar, or governor general, is situated on the left bank of the Blue Nile immediately above its con-
fluence with the White Nile. "The town was built in 1823–30 by Mohammed Ali.
. . . During the rebellion of the Mahdi (Mohammed Ahmed) General Gordon, who
was dispatched hither by the British government to withdraw the garrisons in the
Sudan, entered the town in Feb., 1884 and defended it until Jan. 26th, 1885. The
town was reduced to ruins by the Mahdists, but has been rebuilt since the capture
of Omdurman in 1898. . . . The Gordon Memorial College is a large and substantial building in which native youths are trained by English and Arabic teachers for
an official career. . . . The gardens and villas of the British officials add a picturesque feature to the scene. . . . Gordon's house, in which he fell under the lances of
the dervishes, occupied the same site" (ibid., 412–13).

never left us. He and Murphy took us over to visit Omdurman, and had
donkeys waiting to carry us about the town. They showed us the broken
down palace of the Kaliph, and the wall where he threw the arms, legs
or heads of the people who displeased him.[14] We also saw the hut where
Slatin Pasha was imprisoned so long; and the place where they brought
the head of Gordon to show him. It is splendid now to see the stately
house on the Khartoum side, and bearing on the great gate-posts Slatin's
titles and rank. We also saw in Omdurman the tomb of the Mahdi
destroyed by the English because the Arabs were making a fanatical
shrine of it. It was quite disagreeable riding through the streets, as the
men scowled fiercely at us, so differently from the Arabs.[15] On the bank
we saw great piles of gum arabic, which women were sorting over and
putting in sacks. When the Kaliph was in authority, he brought the whole
of his tribe from Kordofan; and we were told that out in the desert there
were fifty thousand of these Africans in little villages, many of them can-
nibals. In fact both Carrie and Eck rode out with Murphy and Mahomet
into the desert one morning and visited one of these villages. One evening
Murphy brought several young English officers and got me to play accom-
paniments for them to sing some ragged old sentimental ballads. But the
most thrilling thing was going to service in the English chapel in Gordon's
palace. From the window nearest us we saw the tablet on the wall telling
that on that spot Gordon had been killed, after looking for months for
help to come from England. Below this was his garden with the rose-
bushes he had planted. About a dozen English officers formed the choir,
and they laid their swords on the floor under their seats; when, at the

14. Lizzie's grisly account of dismembered bodies was echoed in a contemporary
guidebook. "The place of execution under the Khalifa was in the Date Market, and
to the east of it is the pit (Tomb of the Martyrs') into which were thrown the heads
and limbs of the condemned" (ibid., 416).

15. Lizzie expressed discomfort at the array of races and nationalities. A contemporary guidebook described it well: "The warlike oppression of the last decade, the
fanatical enthusiasm for pilgrimages, the desire for plunder and the devastation of
whole provinces have assembled here a confused medley of the most diverse races
and stocks. Bantus and grotesque dwarf negroes, from the W. Sudan, Semitic
and Hamitic tribes from the desert, such as Nuba, Baggara, Kabbabish, Gowameh,
and Kowahleh Arabs; Nubians, Fellahin. To these must be added Egyptians, Syrians, and a few Greeks" (ibid., 415).

end of the service, "God save the King" was sung, each man put his hand on his hip, where his sword would naturally hang. It was quite touching to know that these young fellows would be the only Englishmen there during the dangerous summer; in command of fine Soudanese troops, but with these thousands of fanatical savages around.

The next time we saw Murphy was two years afterward in London. We had heard of him as governor of the province of Sennar in Africa, and he had sent Carrie some lion's teeth and a table made of elephant hide and many other things. She was sitting in our parlor at the Savoy looking out on the Embankment, when some one asked over the telephone if he could see her. It was Murphy, and he dined with us that night but could only eat soft food, as a lion had clawed out most of his teeth, and the wounds were not yet sufficiently healed to have them replaced. He told us some extraordinary adventures, and the next year came to see us in Philadelphia. He gave Eck a good deal of trouble in some ways, but he was a gallant soldier with some fine Irish traits, and I hope he has wiped out his sins by some glorious deeds, and an honorable death in this war.

On Sunday afternoon our Greek friend sent a very sober and solemn Arab servant to show us the way to his house; and each of us took one of the jin-rick-shaws that ladies use there. We were warmly received by the Greek and his Syrian wife, who was quite pretty and wore as a necklace the gold coronet that had belonged to the Kaliph. The Greek said he had bought it from a private soldier who looted it.

We were detained one day at Khartoum by waiting for a hunting party, who had been spending a month in the region around Gondeka.[16] It was a curious sight seeing them arrive and get off their boat. First a quantity of heads and horns were brought up and leaned against the wall for the government game inspectors to see. Then came Mr. Charles Francis Adams[17] with his wife and daughter, a Polish count (who turned out

16. Gondar is in Ethiopia at the headwaters of the Blue Nile.
17. Charles Francis Adams Jr. (1835–1915) was the grandson of John Quincy Adams and husband of Mary Hone Ogden (b. 1843). He was graduated from Harvard University in 1856 and started practicing law in 1858. After attending Lincoln's inauguration in 1861, he returned to Boston in the spring of 1861 and joined the 4th Battalion of Massachusetts Volunteer Militia. Later that year he received a first lieutenant's commission and served with the 1st Massachusetts Cavalry in

to be quite a character) and then an Englishwoman in a very fashionable light dress and a large flowered hat with a deep lace frill, and carrying a small jewel box. She told us afterwards that while her husband was hunting tigers and elephants,[18] she stayed on the boat, reading, washing and ironing, and wearing entirely pajamas. They had quantities of servants and hunters; and two of them carried up a man, who, they said, had the sleeping sickness. They all went down on the train with us, and we were amazed to find that at the stations along the way the telegraph operator and station master, were nephews and sons of the Kaliph, trained and appointed by the English Government with their wonderful talent for managing their colonies.

When we got on the Nile boat at Wady Halfa, they fastened what they called a sandal at the side, upon which the natives who came down with the hunting party lived. It was like a flat boat, and the natives slept and cooked and said their prayers on it. We got off in the morning to go into the temple of Abou Simbel, which is the most wonderful and impressive of all, being cut into the solid mountain of rock. At that early hour in the morning a ray of sunlight penetrated the heavy narrow doorway and lighted the altar far back under the mountain, reminding us of the Druid's altar at Stonehenge. But how different the cool, green, wind-swept Salisbury plain with the sky-larks singing, from the hot sultry desert, where the burning golden cataract of sand pours down by the side of the great temple of Abou Simbel; where the gigantic statues of Ramesis cut into

South Carolina. Adams saw action at Gettysburg and Antietam, giving vivid descriptions of the horrors of war that he encountered. Following five years in the military, Adams returned to Boston and became a civic leader and historian. He is remembered for helping to temper Northern attitudes toward secession in general and Gen. Robert E. Lee in particular through his provocative writings about the Civil War. Two years after meeting Lizzie Sinkler Coxe, Adams published a lecture to celebrate the centennial of Robert E. Lee's birth ("Charles Francis Adams," *Dictionary of American Biography,* Base Set, American Council of Learned Societies, 1928–36; reproduced in *Biography Resource Center* [Farmington Hills: Gale Group, 2004], http://galenet.galegroup.com/servlet/BioRC [accessed June 27, 2005]; Charles Francis Adams, *Charles Francis Adams, 1835–1915: An Autobiography* [Boston: Houghton Mifflin, 1916]).

18. Lizzie Coxe knew full well that no tigers existed in Africa; perhaps she mentioned this as an exaggeration of what the woman said.

the mountain, have smiled with a strange mysterious meaning into the region across the Nile for thousands of years. On the shoulder of one of them is a Greek inscription cut by a soldier of Xerxes' army.[19]

When we got down to Luxor we had a wonderful meeting with my nieces, Emily and Elizabeth. They had come over from America with the Chapmans and Mrs. Dickson, who kindly looked after them and put them on the night train at Cairo to join us at Luxor. We wanted them at least to see Karnak and as our boat would only tarry a few hours at Luxor, I engaged a nice dragoman we knew there to have several donkeys ready, and a Victoria for myself. George, our Coptic dragoman from the boat, sat on the box his wrist tattooed with the cross. When I got to the station, I found an enormous dragoman in particularly gorgeous attire walking about the platform with a yellow telegram fluttering in his hand. It was from Jean Dickson telling him to meet the girls. Presently the low, queer looking train drew up, with blue glasses, the girls jumped out full of excitement, and in half a minute, they were mounted on the donkeys with Carrie and Eck and Mary Jane, and the whole pack of donkeys and donkey boys, and were off at full gallop for Karnak, their veils flying behind them and fly rushes waving.

One day on our way down the Nile, nearly everyone had gone on shore to see the inscriptions at Tel el Amarna, and Mr. Adams and I were left alone all day sitting on deck and talking about the Civil War and the South.[20] He seemed much interested in hearing about my nieces'

---

19. Built by Rameses II in Nubia on the west bank of the Nile, the temple was first discovered and opened by G. B. Belzoni in 1817. "The temple was built in such a way that twice a year when the rising sun appeared above the horizon on the east bank of the Nile, its rays penetrated the temple entrance shot through the great hall with eight pillars in the form of colossal statues of the king, the second pillared hall, the vestibule and the sanctuary, and rested on the four statues in the niche at the back which they fully illuminated" (John Baines and Jaromir Malek, *Atlas of Ancient Egypt* [New York: Facts on File, 1980], 184).

20. The tombs of el Amarna are some of the most remarkable in Egypt in that they cast light on the daily life of ancient Egypt, such as how granaries were built, how cattle sheds were constructed, and how individual homes might have looked. "A little to the south of Bersheh, at a point where the eastern chain of hills retreats somewhat, we find some most remarkable ruins, the remains of the city and tombs of Tell el Amarna." This was the location of the palaces and temples of the

grandfathers, and was very nice about the South, but did not tell me that he was Colonel of the first regiment that entered Richmond after the surrender. Nor did he mention that all the way down from Khartoum on the train, he had been writing his fine paper on General Lee.

One night on the Nile just before the warning for putting out the lights, the manager of the boat came to Eck, and told him that a felucca[21] had been following us all afternoon and that a man on it had asked for him, and to be taken on board. It was our friend Harry Green, and a delightful traveling companion he proved, for he remained with us until we got back to America.

We stopped at Shepherd's in Cairo and the girls enjoyed the social life as well as the sights and wonders of Egypt. One evening we took them to a fancy ball at the Savoy, and as we sat looking on at all the queer figures, a tall man in a long white cloak and hood, and ghastly white mask, with spurs and boots showing beneath his cloak, thus betraying the fact that he was a cavalry officer, came and bowed before Elizabeth, holding out his hand to invite her to dance. She was terrified and hid her face on my shoulder, though I encouraged her to accept for the fun of it, and he kept holding out his hands imploringly. Finally he gave her a rose, which she

---

Egyptian king Amenhotep IV, who introduced the worship of the sun as the one god. He changed his old name, containing the name of Amon, to Chu-en-'eten, the "splendour of the disk," and moved his capital to Tell el Amarna. "When King Chuen-'eten left the residence of his fathers and founded the town of the 'Horizon of the Sun' in Middle Egypt, for himself and his god, he took care that there should be splendid temple-buildings in his new city, and one of his faithful courtiers, the high priest Meryrê' has, in the pictures of his tomb, transmitted to posterity the story of their grandeur" (Adolf Erman, *Life in Ancient Egypt,* trans. H. M. Tirard 1894; reprint, with a new introduction by Jon Manchip White; [New York: Dover Publications, 1971], 24, 46–47, 286–87). This famous site was the short-lived capital of Egypt and the royal residence during much of the reign of King Akhenaten. "Although it has produced a number of famous works of art, for the visitor el-Amarna is disappointing because there are hardly any buildings standing. The spoliation started soon after the town was abandoned" (John Baines and Jaromir Malek, *Atlas of Ancient Egypt* [New York: Facts on File, 1980], 123–24). Note that in Lizzie's day the area was called Tell el Amarna, while today it is termed el-Amarna.

21. A felucca is a narrow sailing vessel used to travel on the River Nile.

offered to pin on his cloak when he came up as we were going, and he knelt at her feet dramatically while she did so.

When we got back to Naples there was a railroad strike and a great deal of violence, when they ran trains protected by soldiers. For some days no tickets were sold at all. Then they began taking as many passengers as could be protected by the soldiers and as we were anxious to get to Rome before Easter, I told Eck we would risk it. Then it was that Harry Green proved a true friend. In those days of few automobiles he found one that had brought a party from Rome, and urged our taking it. He insisted upon going by train himself to take our trunks, and was so urgent that we accepted, although I now feel it was very selfish to allow this. He knew the car would barely hold our own party, and I was ungrateful enough to be quite angry when he insisted upon this plan. It was such a beautiful ride, too, going through Capua, Terracini, and so many picturesque little towns, over the Campagna and Appian Way to Rome.[22] I shall never forget another instance of Harry Green's unselfishness either. He had been intensely interested in a concert to be given by a splendid company, who were to sing the Ninth Symphony. Not knowing this, Eck asked him to help him take the girls to see Vesuvius, as he could not do it alone. So he said that if Carrie and I would use his tickets for the concert he would be delighted to go. The worst of it was that instead of admiring the scenery

22. "Terracina. This city, the last of the Roman state in this direction, was built by the Volsci who called it Auxur; It was named Trachina (steep) by the Greeks and from this word it derives its present name. . . . The chain of mountains near the city is separated from the Appennines by the extensive valley of the Sacco which is filled with springs that issue from the mountain sides and fall into the marshes. The ancient Romans possessed villas on the hill of Terracina; . . . The Appian way passed through this town; a part of it enclosed within a building belonging to the church is well preserved. The blocks of stone, in the shape of irregular pentagons, are joined with the same exactness as a work of recent date." "Capua. It appears by Strabo that Capua was founded by the Tyrrhenians when they were drive by the Gauls from the line of the Po 542 years before the Christian era. . . . It was founded by Capys, one of the companions of Aeneas from whom it derived its name. . . . The city was celebrated for its situation, the fertility and beauty of the surrounding country styled by Cicero the finest territory of the Roman people. . . . The Via Appia passed through Capua" (Luigi Piale, *Hand-book or New Guide to Naples, Sicily, and the Environs* [Rome: L. Piale, 1853], 9–16).

while driving there, those wretched girls forced Harry to quarrel about North and South all the way. Eck said in vain he tried to draw their attention to the wonderful street scenes, the making of macaroni, the Misericordia Brothers carrying a bier, the glimpses of the Bay of Naples through beautiful old doorways—all they wanted was to force the poor young man, who didn't care a straw about the civil war, to fight its battles over with them.

Lizzie's letters gave a firsthand account of the appearance of Khartum under British rule. They also showed her attitude toward British benevolent paternalism. She believed that the Arabs and blacks of Khartum were much better off with British improvements than they might have been under the Kaliph or Mahdi. She noted that March was late in the season to be in the middle of the Nubian desert. Though she was a seasoned traveler, she suffered from the intense desert heat and the sand storms, and she longed for the patter of rain. It was at Lizzie's invitation that Anne and Emily traveled from the South Carolina Low Country to Luxor to be with their aunt. The young girls called Lizzie "Auntie." Emily was to marry Nicholas Guy Roosevelt[23] and lived between Gippy Plantation[24] in Moncks Corner, South Carolina, and the Highlands in Ambler, Pennsylvania. Anne was to marry Kershaw Fishburne and live in Pinopolis, S.C.

Grand Hotel Khartoum[26]

March 10, 1905

Dearest Wharton,

    It is too queer to be here and more oriental and barbaric than anything you can imagine, although they call it a modern town and a "luxurious"

---

23. Nicholas Guy Roosevelt (1883–1965) was the son of Nicholas Latrobe Roosevelt (1847–1892) and Eleanor Dean (1852–1933), both from New York.

24. According to Anne Sinkler Fishburne, "Gippy Plantation . . . was so named after a local swamp where an old Negro named Gippy, an inveterate runaway, used to hide out in a hollow tree (*Belvidere: A Plantation Memory* [Columbia: University of South Carolina Press, 1950], 55).

25. Anne, who also went with Lizzie on the 1910 trip on the Orient Express, married William Kershaw Fishburne on April 14, 1910.

26. Here was a description of the Grand Hotel from a contemporary travel guide: "Grand Hotel Khartum, German manager, belonging to the London & Soudan

hotel, etc, and really are building very handsome government buildings. The governor's Palace, built on the site of Gordon's, is very fine and in the midst of a tropical garden. There is the Gordon Memorial College and a large hospital and English and Egyptian barracks all built on the high bank of the Blue Nile.[27] All have gardens or rather groves of palms, oleanders, acacias and pride of India and sakiyehs with buffaloes bring up water to irrigate them. This hotel too is on the same high bank with fine verandahs and garden and from our verandah we look over the river and the modern town strung along it to illimitable extents of desert on both sides.

We arrived here this morning after two nights and one day on the train and although we each had a compartment on the sleeper the therm. stood at 98 and the electric fan in two of ours broke down. The sand sifted in through every crack and the route all yesterday went through a truly appalling desert, scattered with white bones and sprinkled with graves. From the white cross and white cast enclosure of the English Officers many single graves to irregular groups of black or red stones stuck up. Like our Bad Lands there is a great deal of volcanic formation, jagged and picturesque lines of hills and desolate black boulders and small stones sprinkled over the red desert sand. When the line ran near the Nile there were palms and lupine patches and mud villages and beehive huts of the Baggaras or Gougolans. But for miles the desert had only dry grey camel thorn and tufts of yellow grass and was a horrible sight filling one with thoughts of suffering and cruelty.

We crossed the fine bridge over the Atbara built by our Pencoyd co of Philadelphia but even the pride in that was marred by the small grave yard

---

Development Co., a long building in the bungalow style on the Blue Nile, commanding a fine view, with airy rooms, and a small dependence situated in a pretty garden; pension from 1 pound per day. Invalids are recommended to select the rooms at the back, which are less exposed to the north wind, though destitute of view" (Karl Baedeker, *Egypt and the Sudan* [Leipzig: Karl Baedeker, 1908], 411).

27. "Along the bank of the Nile runs the embankment, a promenade about 3 miles in length, planted with palms and other trees. At its eastern extremity lies the hamlet of Burri, and as we proceed thence towards the west we pass successively the British Barracks, a fragment of the old town wall, the Gordon Memorial College and the Hospital" (ibid., 423).

in which lie some American young men who helped to put it up. We saw in the distance the pyramids of Merve and went through Berber and looked across at Dongola where most of the Dervishes came. Also it was interesting as well as comfortable yesterday morning to take baths at Abou Hamad where Kitchener had them built—porcelain tubs and clean towels in a heavy masonry building but I did not feel clean for more than an hour. The food on the dining car was very good but the ice gave out. Warm apollmums and hot oranges increase one's thirst frightfully, so we are very thankful to get here although there is a fearful sand storm raging. All the windows on that side are shut tight but everything is covered with a thick layer and the ink writes gritty. The Khamsin[28] is much more dreaded than heat, but I prefer this cool air even thick with sand.

We were the only ladies on the train and only two are left at this hotel. Last week they had the therm at 100 for days and Lady Wingate has gone to Cairo, and most of the other officers wives probably. However, I trust by making our excursions very early in the morning we shall not get sick, and I see they have rickshaws drawn by donkeys which I expect to save one a great deal. Our only companions in this end of the season trip are a stout old Englishman of 76 with a stalwart young Irish companion, and a German "counselor." There were two other youths but they got off at Berber for hunting.[29] Mr. Prance, the Englishman, has been the wonder of the Nile boat. Although very infirm he never missed anything one could crawl into or climb up to and put on dress clothes every night. There were several English officers on the train and a Greek merchant—very gentlemanly who has asked us to take tea with his wife on Sunday afternoon.

---

28. Khamsin, khamseen, or camsim is "an oppressive hot wind from the south or south-east, which in Egypt blows at intervals for about 50 days in March, April, and May, and fills the air with sand from the desert" ("Khamsin," *Oxford English Dictionary Online*, http://dictionary.oed.com/ [accessed July 12, 2005]).

29. Big-game hunting was one of the prime attractions of Upper Nubia: "Excellent shooting may be enjoyed in the Sudan. . . . An ordinary shooting license costs 5 pounds per annum. The right to shoot buffaloes, elephants, hippopotami, various large antelopes, ostriches, and various other large birds (such as the ibis, marabou stork, and flamingo) costs 25 pounds per annum besides a special fee for each animal bagged. Giraffes may not be killed at all" (Karl Baedeker, *Egypt and the Sudan* [Leipzig: Karl Baedeker, 1908], 407).

Eck is as pleased and interested as he expected, but I must confess I shall be thankful to get off on Tuesday. As the mail is going and there is no other for four days will you mind sending to Charlie.

Your devoted, L. Much love to all.

Grand Hotel Khartoum
Sudan
March 13, 1905

Dearest Charlie,

I found on Friday after I had written to Wharton that the mail was just going and no other for four days so I asked him to send you mine telling our journey here. Have just had the delight of letters from home. After getting none for 10 days and now have two from Mary, one from Becky and a delightful one from Anne. I have not heard a line from you since before we sailed and do hope you will write sometimes for I miss greatly not hearing from you.

These continued accounts of severe cold from Anne as well as from Philadelphia seem too queer as it has been summer with us for so long. However we are too grateful here for the heat to be so mitigated by a violent north wind that the therm has gone down to 80 after standing at over 100 for a week before we arrived. As I wrote Wharton this hotel is delightfully situated on the Blue Nile on a high bank on the same line with the Sirdar's palace. The Gordon Memorial College where the sons of his old enemies are being educated form barracks and other public buildings all surrounded by what are called gardens, that is groups of palms towering above oleanders and other flowering shrubs which are irrigated by Sakiyehs, and beyond that on all sides nothing but desert of a reddish colour from which comes occasionally gusts and clouds of sand. Through glasses you can see the desert is dotted with mud or straw villages all the same colour. Eck has gone out on a donkey this morning with our Dragoman Mohammed to see some of these villages of all sorts of tribes. Mohammed is a good looking young Arab and was in the English army and fought in the battle of Omdurman only 6 years ago. It is really marvelous all the English have done since then, for Khartoum has been entirely built as I have described and here are ferrys and steam launches, soldier policemen and every thing under military rule—Sanitation, transportation, etc.

*Elizabeth Sinkler
Coxe (1843–1919)*

*Charles Brinton Coxe, Sr.
(1843–1873)*

*Eckley Brinton Coxe, Jr.
(1872–1916)*

Eckley Brinton Coxe, Jr., and Elizabeth Sinkler Coxe at Windy Hill

Elizabeth Sinkler Coxe on the porch at Windy Hill

Above and next page: the house at Windy Hill and the workmen who built it, 1895

Wharton Sinkler, Sr. (1845–1910)

Fish Pond Windy Hill

Above and next page: the garden at Windy Hill, 1900

*Emily Wharton Sinkler
Roosevelt (1884–1970),
Lizzie's niece*

*Laura Ann Stevens
Manning (1889–1988),
left, and Anne Wickham
Sinkler Fishburne
(1886–1983), right,
Lizzie's nieces*

Belvidere Plantation, 1900. Lizzie's Southern home

Plantation Life
circa 1900-1916

Plantation life at Belvidere

The Battery at Charleston, 1900

Lizzie at the Belvidere back gate

Rameses—
R Hydro
On the Nile

PAGNON'S LUXOR HOTEL

LUXOR (UPPER EGYPT)

Feb. 21st 1895

Dearest Anne— It is seldom that
I can find a day to write to you,
when Carry has not just sent you
a letter— but she & Leh have
gone on a day's excursion, & I have
a wee idle time to write, & so
will risk repeating things.
Neither Carry nor I felt very well
last night & decided not to take
the trip today, as it is 2 hours to the
Tombs and back on donkeys. This
morning when we found a me...

Stationery from Pagnon's Luxor Hotel (above) and Shepheard's Hotel, Cairo (next page), 1895

Shepheard's Hotel, Cairo

Ph. Zech,
Propr:
Electric light. Hydraulic lifts.

Telegraphic Address:

SHEPHEARDS CAIRO.

March 1ˢᵗ 1895

Dearest Anna —

Although I love
to write to you at all
times, one sometimes feels
discouraged at the thought
that we are really too far
apart for a regular answering
interchange of letters. If you
could see how eagerly welcomed
your letters are by us, you
would be pleased — you put the
every day recurrences in such
a vivid & cheerful light that
it is so delightful. Although
there is so much ahead of us,

Our visit to Omdurman on Saturday was deeply interesting. We saw the Khalifa's house of the capture of which you will see such a thrilling account in "With Kitchener to Khartoum," the Mahdi's Tomb and Slatin Pasha's hut and the barracks where the Camel Corps and the Mule Corps are composed of the Dervishes who survived. Those who are soldiers look busy and contented but in the bazaars and markets we saw many fierce and sullen black faces peering from the folds of their white burnoose. The Khalifa's tribe of Baggnras were mostly sent back to Korbofan but the English have wisely kept all the prominent men and the children of the Khalifa and Mahdi under surveillance educating them and giving them positions as clerks in the post offices and stations, etc. If you were here you would enjoy going on hunts with some of the officers I know, but Eck you know doesn't care for shooting. Interesting and wonderful as it is here I shall be too glad to turn our faces north tomorrow for it has been such a dread to me that one of us might get ill and be detained in this far away place, 1500 miles from Cairo even, and in a little oasis of civilization that seems only skin deep. We continually plan and think about the girls expected arrival this day week in Cairo. I am too delighted to think of their having the experience of seeing even a little of wonderful Egypt. By the bye Anne does not speak of your getting the rain coat I sent you. I hope there was no mistake.

Your devoted Lizzie

I hate to think of you and Anne having only darling little Cadsy with you. I wish you would let Anne come a little earlier.

> Cook's Nile Steamer Services
> S.S. Rameses The Great
> Luxor
> March 22, 1905

Dearest Anne and Charlie,

The girls have arrived! And are well and safe and looking splendidly! This morning at 8:30 Carrie, Eck and I with a carriage, 4 donkeys, 4 donkey boys and 2 dragomen[30] went to the station to meet them. There we

---

30. A dragoman was an interpreter, chiefly of the Arabic language, and was employed in the Near East.

found Cook had sent their finest dragoman also as a telegram had arrived, "send special man to meet two young ladies Sinkler."[31] The kind Chapmans sent us two telegrams last night and fearing there might be some mistake Mrs. Dikson sent this to Cook too. I have not heard why the others did not come up.

We mounted them on donkeys at once with Carrie and Eck and Shemandi and they galloped off to see Karnak as our boat leaves at 11. We have a lovely big cabin for them next to Cad's and I am sure the four days on this beautiful river will more than pay them for the night train. It is too beautiful and the weather perfect—full moon too. I am too glad we took the trouble to write so many letters to them and the Chapmans and so many telegrams, as it explained why they had to come by this morning or lose Luxor and the Nile.

You would have been too happy to see the scene at the station. All the Dragomen and soldiers laughed with joy as they saw the meeting. Such screams of joy and hugs and kisses that waving palms have rarely witnessed. And now M.J. has their bags unpacked and I am waiting for them on deck.

For much love to Cadsy and you, your devoted L

31. The two young ladies were Anne and Charlie Sinkler's two oldest daughters. Emily Wharton Sinkler later married Nicholas Guy Roosevelt on April 15, 1916, and lived at the Highlands in Ambler, Pennsylvania. Anne Wickham Sinkler later married William Kershaw Fishburne. Anne (this author's grandmother) took over the management of Belvidere for her father, Charles, and when Belvidere was inundated by the damming of the Santee River in 1942, Anne and Kershaw Fishburne moved to Pinopolis, South Carolina. Lizzie remembers being accompanied by Emily Sinkler and Elizabeth Stevens. In actuality she was accompanied by Emily and Anne Sinkler. Perhaps Elizabeth accompanied her on another trip to Egypt.

CHAPTER SIX

Underwriting Excavations in Nubia, 1909

Lizzie and Eck were regular visitors to Egypt. This fascination with the country resulted in Eck's growing financial and organizational involvement with the University of Pennsylvania's museum excavations.

This was an active time in the exploration of Egypt. From 1880 until the First World War, the English and French were heavily involved in the governmental and cultural affairs of Egypt. Ancient Egypt was a new area of discovery for Westerners. Egypt was ruled at the end of the eighteenth century by the Mamelukes. The monuments of ancient Egypt were buried by sand until their rediscovery in the early years of the nineteenth century. The language seemed inscrutable: "Generally speaking, ancient Egypt was both remote and incomprehensible; by definition, hieroglyphic was priestly carving, and priests are always suspected of cabalistic mysteries. Therefore, the hieroglyphs must be supercharged with secret symbolism; they could not be read as a Westerner might read Arabic or Chinese."[1]

Without any comprehension of the writing of ancient Egypt, there was little appreciation for the ancient monuments. This changed dramatically with the decipherment of hieroglyphic writing by the Frenchman Jean-François Champollion in 1822. Champollion used the Rosetta Stone, unearthed in Napoleon's 1798 expedition to Egypt, as a guide to the ancient language. The stone was a trilingual text of Greek, Demotic script of early Egypt, and hieroglyphs. Hieroglyphics were in use in ancient Egypt from

1. John A. Wilson, *Signs & Wonders upon Pharaoh: A History of American Egyptology* (Chicago: University of Chicago Press, 1964), 11.

about 3000 B.C.E. to 250 C.E. The sophisticated language and writing combined picture writing with the rebus principle that a picture of something might stand for its sound rather than for itself. Once the language was understood, the entire history of Egypt lay open in hundreds of texts on temples, tombs, monuments, and in papyrus rolls.

The ancient monuments that had seemed inscrutable became a passion for French, British, and American explorers. Many ruthless adventurers undertook to unearth the ancient treasures. Giovanni Belzoni, sponsored by the British, unearthed the great head of Rameses II and shipped it back to England. He discovered and unearthed the temple at Abu Simbel and the tomb of Seti I in the Valley of the Kings. Belzoni's methods were those of the plunderer, not the archaeologist. "Belzoni turned his attention to the Valley of the Kings at Thebes and uncovered four tombs, with mummies and mummy cases. If a blocked-up doorway confronted him, he fashioned a battering ram and knocked a hole in it, without regard to any seal-impressions which might be on it or to any objects which might have been immediately behind it. When he first penetrated a passage of a tomb, he said, 'Every step I took I crushed a mummy in some part or other.'"[2]

In 1806 Mohammed Ali, a Macedonian, had conquered Egypt and was recognized by the Turks as the pasha of Egypt. He ruled Egypt until 1841. During that time he attempted to gain control of the foreign expeditions that were plundering Egyptian monuments. His method of issuing a "firman" to excavate or conduct research only put a stamp of authority on the wholesale collecting of Egyptian antiquities for purchase. This continued under Mohammed Ali's son, Said Pasha, and his grandson, Khedive Ismail, who ruled until he was deposed by the British in 1879. Order was imposed on the freewheeling British and French explorers by Khedive Said's appointment in 1858 of the Frenchman Auguste Mariette as Conservator of Egyptian Monuments, a post he held until 1881. "Mariette's work concentrated on some of the most exciting places in Egypt: the Serapeum and the mastaba tombs at Sakkara; the handsome temple of Seti I at Abydos; three of the greatest temples in the Theban area, Karnak, Deir el-Bahari, and Medinet Habu; and the great Ptolemaic temple to Horus at Edfu."[3] Mariette

2. Ibid., 28.
3. Ibid., 47.

founded a national museum for Egyptian antiquities and brought to an end the ruthless exploitation of Belzoni and others.

Archaeology was a new field in 1880. It was dominated by the talented British archaeologist Sir Flinders Petrie,[4] and an American, George Reisner, who was sponsored by the Boston Museum of Fine Arts and Harvard University. This was the beginning of scientific archaeology in Egypt. Petrie aimed to reconstruct the totality of Egyptian society by combining textual and well-documented archaeological data. He used these data to weave a history out of the scattered evidence of inscriptions and objects.[5]

Lizzie and Eckley participated in this exciting new age of Egyptian exploration. They had visited Egypt, as evidenced by their trips in 1895 and 1905. Eckley Coxe learned to appreciate exacting field methods, involving the systematic removal of earth, meticulous recording at all stages of a dig, and careful supervision of Egyptian workers. Eckley Coxe graduated from the University of Pennsylvania in 1893 and had no special qualifications except wealth and his interest in Egypt.

The University of Pennsylvania had maintained an interest in Egyptian archaeology since a scholarly group in 1856 undertook a new translation of the Rosetta Stone.[6] The Egyptian section of the University Museum was established in 1890 with Sara Yorke Stevenson as director. The museum engaged David Randall-MacIver and Charles Leonard Woolley. Both MacIver and Woolley were to become close friends of Lizzie and Eckley.

In 1910 Eckley Brinton Coxe Jr. became president of the board of the University Museum. He was assisted by George Byron Gordon, director of the museum. Under Coxe's stewardship the museum began important excavations in Upper Nubia at Buhen.[7] The site was near the Second Cataract. MacIver and Woolley's camp during the 1907–10 expeditions was

4. "Sir William Matthew Flinders Petrie (1853–1942), the Egyptian and Palestinian archaeologist, was one of the most extraordinary of the great polymaths of his period" (Margaret Drower, ed. *Letters from the Desert: The Correspondence of Flinders and Hilda Petrie* [Oxford: Aris and Phillips, 2004], viii).

5. David O'Connor and David Silverman, "The University Museum in Egypt," *Expedition,* 21 (Winter 1979): 17.

6. John A. Wilson, *Signs & Wonders upon Pharaoh: A History of American Egyptology* (Chicago: University of Chicago Press, 1964), 58.

7. David O'Connor and David Silverman, "The University Museum in Egypt," *Expedition,* 21 (Winter 1979): 21.

situated near Wadi Halfa. Lizzie and Eck visited the camp in April 1909, and Eck designed a hot-water shower for their use at the camp.

Upper Nubia was a new area for exploration.[8] Upper Nubia was an unusual province of ancient Egypt because of its frontier position between Egypt and other important African groups. MacIver and Woolley excavated communities as well as cemeteries. Two seasons were spent excavating the Egyptian fortress town at Buhen, which dated to the Middle and New Kingdoms (ca. 2000–1000 B.C.E.). MacIver and Woolley uncovered the Meroitic civilization of Upper Nubia. The excavations showed that this second- to fourth-centuries C.E. society lived in brick towns and villages linked to the great Meroitic kingdom of the Sudan. MacIver discovered the tomb of an Egyptianized Nubian chieftain, Hekanefer, of the fourteenth century B.C.E., and in 1910 discovered at Buhen statuettes of Amenemhat a fifteenth-century B.C.E. Egyptianized chief.[9]

"Coxe's enthusiasm for Egyptological research remained undimmed after MacIver's departure. In 1914 Director Gordon, with Coxe's financial backing, recruited a new Egyptian curator, Clarence Stanley Fisher."[10] Coxe provided the financial support for Fisher's excavations in Memphis.

8. "At this time David Randall-MacIver (1873–1945) and Charles Leonard Woolley (1880–1960), working for the University Museum and the University of Pennsylvania's Eckley B. Coxe Jr. Expedition, excavated a number of important sites in Nubia, including a small fortified encampment belonging to a late phase of the C-Group culture at Areika. The site covered less than an acre, and within its walls were areas for grain storage, mills, and ovens. Among the artifacts discovered were the typical black incised bowls of the C-Group as well as objects imported from Egypt or strongly influenced by Egyptian wares. The most impressive site explored by the Coxe expedition was the great fortress of Buhen, one of the largest and most imposing of the mud-brick fortifications built as a chain in the early Middle Kingdom to guard Egypt's Nubian frontier. Its defensive walls fronted by a deep dry moat measured more than a mile in length. Inside were the houses of soldiers as well as temples built of stone dating from the New Kingdom reuse of the site. From 1908 to 1910 Randall-MacIver and Woolley uncovered a number of cemeteries dating from the Middle Kingdom through the New Kingdom and recorded the plans of the battlements and the decorated walls of the temples" (Nancy Thomas, ed., *The American Discovery of Ancient Egypt* [Los Angeles: Los Angeles County Museum of Art, 1996], 142–43).

9. Ibid., 28.

10. Ibid.

Fisher's expedition of 1915–20 uncovered the remains of a large mud-brick palace of the pharaoh Merenptah (ca. 1236–1223 B.C.E.), and totally cleared a large area of stratified ancient town remains running over the palace ruins and surrounding them on every side. With Coxe financing, Fisher began excavations in the cemetery of Dendera, a cult center to the goddess Hathor. Fisher uncovered over two thousand tombs.

As president of the museum board, Eckley Coxe took his administrative responsibilities seriously. "From 1905 Coxe paid for the salaries of MacIver, Woolley and for Fisher, for their expeditions and for the costs of the Egyptian Section. . . . Coxe visited Buhen in 1909 and with MacIver's advice, undertook excavations there himself. . . . Coxe's death in 1916 did not end, but rather ensured the Museum's Egyptological research, for he left an endowment of $500,000 which was primarily for the Egyptian Section."[11]

British hegemony dominated the Egypt that was the favorite winter pilgrimage point for Lizzie and Eckley.[12] In July of 1882 the British placed Egypt under a protectorate, keeping Khedive Taufik in a titular position. Sir Evelyn Baring, known as Lord Cromer, became consul general of Egypt in 1883, and from this post he ruled Egypt until 1901. Cromer's greatest difficulty came from the Mahdi of the Sudan, who with his band of Dervishes or Mahdists captured Khartum and assassinated the British general Gordon in January 1885. Lizzie and Eck visited Khartum in 1895, only five years after the Battle of Omdurman, in which the British wrested control of the Sudan from the Mahdi.

The Egypt that Lizzie and Eck had visited beginning in the 1890s was the watering hole for wealthy British and European visitors. Lizzie wrote many letters from Shepheard's Hotel in Cairo. It was the focal point for the winter social scene. "From Shepheard's famous terrace, over a coffee or a

---

11. Ibid., 44.
12. "The best months for Egypt are from October to May. The weather is delightful all through. In the worst years indeed one may possibly count ten days that are not quite perfect, but a few showers, one or two days of rain, and perhaps one day of rather hot wind and dust in April are all one need expect. The rest is sunshine and warmth such as even the Riviera cannot afford. Of routes there is a very wide choice: One can go by long sea, which takes from twelve to fifteen days and is certainly cheapest, or one may go from Marseilles, Genoa, Naples, Venice, Trieste, Brindisi or Constantinople" (A. O. Lamplough, *Egypt and How to See It* [New York: Doubleday, Page, 1907], 11).

lemon squash, one could sit idly and watch the teeming throng sweep past: Egyptians in from the villages returning one's stare openly, barefooted Nubians of great dignity, two-wheeled donkey carts, and then shouts and a rumble as an open landau carrying some fat Turkish dignitary in a red *tarbush*[13] careened past, preceded by running *saises,* who cleared the way with sticks. Veiled ladies rode by, fiercely guarded by eunuchs. A diplomatic carriage would have a fiercely moustached *kavass*[14] mounted beside the driver and clothed in brilliant costume and carrying a curved saber and staff as insignia of his master's sublimity. "He who plunged into the 'native city' . . . had need of a stout stick to keep off the beggars, peddlers, importunists of various pleasures and bargains, and dogs. . . . One needed a good bath on return to the hotel."[15]

After visiting in Cairo, Lizzie and Eck would take one of Cook's Nile Service steamers, usually the *Rameses the Great* up the Nile to visit Assiut, Abydos, Luxor, Aswan, Philae and Abu Simbel. The river was full of beautiful white-winged Egyptian feluccas, and also with many personal dahabiyehs, a commodious sailing houseboat. Cook's Nile Service provided these personal dahabiyehs, which had cabins, dining salons, bathrooms, and an observation lounge. "A huge triangular sail was toward the prow and a lesser sail mounted astern. It was a thrilling sight to see one of these 'golden things' sweeping up the river with a favorable wind."[16]

This travel account gave graphic descriptions of Eck's camp life at Buhen in Lower Nubia, where the University of Pennsylvania Museum was in the midst of excavations. The trip began in February with the crossing on the *Caronia,*[17] stopping first at Madeira. From there the ship docked at both

13. A tarbush, or tarboosh, is a flat-topped felt cap with a tassel, also known as a fez.

14. A kavass is "an armed constable or police officer, an armed servant or courier (in Turkey)" ("Kavass," *Oxford English Dictionary Online,* http://dictionary.oed.com/ [accessed July 12, 2005]).

15. John A. Wilson, *Signs & Wonders upon Pharaoh: A History of American Egyptology* (Chicago: University of Chicago Press, 1964), 73.

16. Ibid., 74.

17. RMS *Caronia,* "launched on 13 July 1904, was built for Cunard by John Brown & Co., of Glasgow. She left Liverpool on her maiden voyage to New York on 25 February 1905" (http://www.greatships.net/caronia.html [accessed March

Genoa and Naples on the way to Cairo. There the party boarded the *Rameses the Great* steamer for a trip up the Nile with Cook's Nile Service.

The party consisted of Lizzie, her niece Emily Sinkler, son Eckley, who had just been made president of the board of the University of Pennsylvania Museum, and George Byron Gordon, the new director of the museum. The party was met at Aswan by David Randall-MacIver, the chief curator for the museum's archaeological digs in Buhen. The assistant curator, Woolley, was also part of the team. The group traveled by boat from Cairo, stopping first at Esna, a major Greco-Roman site. From there they journeyed up the Nile from Aswan to the Second Cataract for their destination, Wadi Halfa and the camp-site at Buhen.

The museum's digs in this area were extensive, employing over eighty workers. MacIver "had established the Museum as a major excavator in Egypt. . . . Coxe, an Egyptological enthusiast, provided funds for a curatorial staff and excavations. MacIver believed that Lower Nubia as the frontier of Ancient Egypt had great potential archaeologically. . . . During the first year in Nubia, MacIver discovered a rich provincial culture with strong connections with Late Roman and Byzantine Egypt. . . . In 1907–08 he excavated a settlement of the C-group, the indigenous Lower Nubian culture from ca. 2290 B.C. This settlement clearly reflected the increasing influence of Egyptian architectural norms. . . . On a much larger scale was the great Egyptian fortress town at Buhen which dated to the Middle and new Kingdoms (ca. 2000–1000 B.C.E.) Two seasons were spent at Buhen, one of the best preserved examples of ancient military architecture in the Near East, and much data of great historical value was collected."[18]

Lizzie gave a vivid description of camp life at Buhen. Each member of the party had his or her own little bungalow. Cooking was done over a small charcoal stove. Dr. MacIver did much of the cooking. The heat was often intense. Eck had designed a hot water shower for the camp, and hot water was brought each morning for baths. The conditions were primitive. Lizzie and her niece Emily and sister Carrie wore long dresses, making the

---

26, 2004]). *Caronia* was the ship that sent the iceberg warning the night *RMS Titanic* sunk in 1912.

18. David O'Connor and David Silverman, "The University Museum in Egypt," *Expedition*, 21 (Winter 1979): 20–21.

heat difficult to bear. Lizzie seemed to thrive on the adventure. The trip ended with an excursion to Italy with Woolley, whose knowledge of Italian architecture and archaeology added considerably to their pleasure.

It was on this trip that young Emily Sinkler made the lifelong friendship of the young British Captain Bassett who held the title of Bimbashi.[19] He gave her a wonderful scarab little-finger ring etched with hieroglyphics, which she wore her entire life. It eventually came into the possession of this author. The relationship was mentioned briefly in the single letter that exists from this trip.

The letter also reveals that Lizzie and her party were moored at Luxor for several days to visit the temples at Karnak and, across the Nile, the tombs at the Valley of the Kings. Lizzie and Eck loved this area and stopped here on every season's trip. In ancient times the city was known as Thebes. The most important temple in Luxor is that erected by Amenhotep III of the Eighteenth Dynasty (1391–1353 B.C.E.) honoring the god Amon. The immense complex had additions under Rameses II (1290–1224 B.C.E.) and Tuthmoses III (1479–1425 B.C.E.). The complex was known for its colonnades with two rows of papyrus capital columns. There are beautiful reliefs depicting the lives of the various Pharaohs. The Luxor temple was linked to the massive Karnak complex by a double row of sphinxes.[20]

Rameses the Great
Cooks Nile Service
March 19, 1909

Dearest Anne,

It has been too delightful to get our first sets of letters from home and you can hardly imagine our longing for more always. I suppose you thought it most prudent not to refer to the two most burning subjects. Wharton's illness has been a great shock and anxiety and Ella's full letter on the subject and all she felt or feared when he arrived in that condition—which I received only yesterday has made it seem even more serious. Of course I

19. *Bimbashi,* or *binbashi,* is a Swahili term for field officer, colonel, or major commandant.
20. Margaret Bunson, *The Encyclopedia of Ancient Egypt* (New York: Facts on File, 1990), 150.

am deeply thankful he is so much better but I do not think we shall ever again feel the same confidence in his health.

Then of course the other subject I feel most interested in is Elizabeth's prospects, which although I am sure is a satisfaction to her and Mary, is also a source of anxiety and complications.[21]

We think more and more of your joining us, and I have written already to the Palace Hotel in Rome for our rooms. We expect to stop at the Grand Hotel in Naples and I shall advise Cook to send you there. By the bye I never knew till Stebbing's letter to me a day or two ago that you could not take steamer of April 10, but although I am sorry, I can easily understand it would be difficult to leave home so early. It is hard to believe in this mid-summer heat that summer has not come with you. Tell Charlie I haven't had a line from him since long before we sailed. Of course dear Anne, the cheques I sent you from New York I intended to enable you to get a good letter of credit by saving you other expenses and for as you know, the expenses of washing, tips and other extras abroad mount up considerably although I have provided for all I could in the itinerary.

I hope Em has told you of the devotion of her young English captain. She flushed so prettily when he met us in the early morning at the station with his bunch of roses and he had written to her twice. The 3 days we spent at Luxor moored to the banks were intensely hot and I minded it all the more on account of my very bad cold and cough which made me obliged to avoid any little breeze that came up. I lost all ambition and did not take one excursion but at 4 this morning the paddle wheels began to churn and we glided out into mid stream with a fresh air and I heard the Arabs singing in their great white winged boats. The Duke of Cornnaught and his royal suite anchored near us last night and were going to see the tombs of the Kings this morning at 6:30. I want to write to Anne.

With love to Charlie, Your devoted, Lizzie

Following is Lizzie's journal entry.

21. Lizzie's youngest sister was Mary Wharton Sinkler (1857–1934), who married Charles Stevens on February 20, 1884. Their eldest daughter was Elizabeth Allen Stevens, born December 31, 1884.

Perhaps the happiest of all these memories is of our visit to Eck's camp at Buhen near Wady Halfa. Everything was so unexpected and exciting and more or less dangerous to my timid mind. We sailed on the *Caronia* straight for Alexandria. Sophy Cadwalader,[22] Emily, and Dr. Gordon went with us, and we took Thomas and Hannah [personal maids] who were great additions. The voyage was extremely pleasant, and we settled down into a very homelike life—having our chairs on deck comfortably arranged at the stern. We sewed and Dr. Gordon read aloud to us Hypatia and Kipling. We stopped a few hours at the Azores, where some of the party went ashore in a small boat that jumped over the waves in too lively a way to suit me. They brought us back all sorts of pretty things—baskets, dolls, and luscious little pineapples.

The next place was Madeira which is a very delightful memory. All afternoon we were passing close to beautiful islands, which are mountains rising out of the sea, and all up the steep sides were sparkling waterfalls and cascades of pink and red bougainvillias and chalets. About sunset we entered the beautiful harbor and soon landed in a small boat and climbed up the steep stone steps which lead to a scene of enchantment.[23] The moon hung overhead and the lights twinkled under the avenue of great sycamore trees where many attractive booths of baskets and embroideries and picturesque cages of parrots hung. Then we saw for the first time their curious sledges like a palanquin with gay calico curtains and cushions mounted on broad runners and drawn by a pair of oxen. A Portuguese walks alongside carrying a greased rag with which he oils the runners from time to time, and the streets are all paved with small pebbles almost like mosaic.[24] But the funny thing was that there were no reins or

22. Sophia "Sophy" Cadwalader (1867–1955) was the daughter of Mary Helen Fisher (1844–1937) and John Cadwalader Jr., an old friend of Charles Brinton Coxe (1843–1873), Lizzie's deceased husband.

23. Madeira and the Canary Islands are just north of the thirtieth parallel and off the coast of West Africa. They were on the direct shipping route from the New World to the Old. The harbor at Madeira is Funchal. The heart of the island is a range of mountains, with St. Antonio rising to 5,706 feet behind the port (A. Samler Brown, *Madeira and the Canary Islands* [London: Sampson, Low, Marston and Co., 1894], 84.

24. "Portuguese is spoken in Madeira and Spanish in the Canaries. . . . Those wishing to take houses, either in Madeira or elsewhere, must be prepared for long

bits and apparently no way of guiding the oxen—but a little ragged boy
with a short stick walked carefully ahead of them, and wherever he went
they went, and if he had run down a steep path to the sea, I supposed we
should have followed. As we drove up in this queer way to the English
Hotel on the heights, we could see in the moonlight through great gate-
ways, gardens with hedges of calla lillies, walls covered with heliotrope
that scented the night-air, and flowers of every delicious kind.[25] At the
English Hotel we met an English friend of Sophy's, who was most kind,
and next day sent me her delightful canvas hammock carried by two
Portuguese in picturesque costumes—for me to use all day, as one would
offer a carriage or gondola, and she also sent us to the steamer the most

---

negotiations. Prices asked of the English in the Canaries are several times as much
as were paid a few years ago. Above all strict enquiries must be made regarding the
supply of water and what chance there is of its being pure. . . . Mosquitoes are
found on the eastern and southern sides of the Canary Islands, especially those
nearest Africa. When present, the night must be passed under curtains. . . . In all
the islands . . . foreigners, especially English people, occasionally suffer from diar-
rhea. . . . Invalids are too apt to imagine that the mere change of climate permits
them to take liberties with their strength and stomach such as they would never
dream of in Europe. Elated and excited by the charm of a nearly constant sunshine
and a temperature which permits them to be out at almost any hour in the day,
they fail to see the necessity of dieting and watching themselves carefully. . . . This
variety of choice, which may at first sight seem to operate against the value of the
islands as a health resort, is as a matter of fact, the one great point in their favour.
Rapidly growing in popularity, they are attracting the attention of physicians of all
nations" (ibid., 4, 5, 6, 7).

25. "Funchal is beautifully situated in a species of vast amphitheatre, the summits
covered with verdure and the sides with villas, gardens, and orchards. The houses
gradually approach one another, form themselves into streets and descend to the
sea level where the dark Lo Rock, the Governor's Palace, the line of houses, the sig-
nal tower, the custom house and the black beach, form a fine contrast to the deep
blue of the arena or sea. The gladiators are replaced by some half dozen ships and
an infinity of little boats, hurrying out to meet some newly arrived steamer or
speeding away the parting guest by endeavouring to sell him a basket deck chair, or
by still smaller boats each containing two little boys shouting and gesticulating for
money to be thrown into the water for them to dive and fetch up. The terraces covered with flowers, here and there a wall crimson with one creeper or orange with
another, the sound of the church bells as a relief from the monotonous four bells
or eight bells on board ship" (ibid., 71).

splendid basket of flowers I ever saw. Next day we tried one of their great
amusements, going up a great height in a switch-back and coming down
on velvet cushioned toboggans—a very dizzy and dangerous sport—as
several were upset. At every house door were women sitting doing their
famous embroidery, but the other famous industry—Madeira wine—
seemed to be hardly heard of.[26]

After leaving this enchanting island, we then had a delightful stop
of a day at Gibraltar, where we went to church, and then lunched with
Emily's cousin, Julia Leigh, who married Captain Greenwood, and they
were stationed there in a delightful house. At Gibraltar they brought on
board all sorts of lace scarfs and gay Eastern shawls and Turkish fezes for
sale, which seemed to inspire the passengers to get up a very amusing
fancy ball. Emily as a Spanish girl, was very charming, and danced with
men of every type and kind. The Captain of the ship was a very jolly
Irishman, who believed all women like attentions and joined her walking
on deck with Dr. Gordon. To her dismay he presently kissed her, which
she pretended not to notice, but made some excuse to go in. Dr. Gordon
said to her, "you saved me from a most disagreeable situation by the dignity with which you ignored that impertinence."

We stopped for a day at beautiful Genoa and after that a day at
Naples where our attention was chiefly given to hot chocolate and cakes
at Cafleschs, as there was no time for anything more important. Then we
passed slowly through the straits of Messina and saw the ruins left by the
great earthquake and finally arrived at Cairo, and stopped at the Semiranis
on the Nile, which was formerly the palace of the Khedive's grandmother.

26. "In the Canaries vines are planted on unirrigated slopes, and find a congenial home amongst volcanic cinders or slag. They have been and will probably again
become the most important of all products of the country. . . . The most approved
manner of growing the vine in Madeira at present is by planting cuttings from
American stock some four feet deep, the soil having previously been turned over to
the same depth. . . . The vines are trained on trellises on the south. . . . A hundred-
weight of grapes should produce about a barril (44 litres) of must which can be
sold to the wine merchants from 8s to 14s per barril. When thought desirable fer-
mentation is checked by the addition of from 5% to 10% of spirit, and the wine is
matured by submitting it to a temperature from 90 to 140 degrees. . . . Madeira is
shipped at an average strength of 32 degree sykes of proof spirit . . . and the chief
consumers are the French, Germans and Russians" (ibid., 216–17).

In a few days we joined Eck and Dr. Gordon at Esna, where they had preceded us by boat.[27] They were burnt a deep red brown and had bad coughs which they were quite unaware of. This is where the beautiful silver scarfs are made and also lovely pottery. Finally, we reached Aswan where Dr. MacIver came to meet us, full of excitement and interest at having us for guests at the Camp. We had intended leaving Hannah and Thomas at Aswan but he insisted on our bringing them as he said it would be the greatest relief to his mind, if Hannah would not mind sleeping in their dark photography room.[28] Of course our dear Hannah did not mind and I was too thankful to have her. We took the boat at Shellal for the 2nd Cataract and Dr. MacIver had a corner of the deck piled with tin bath tubs, boxes of water and bottles and all sorts of mysterious packages.[29] At Wady Halfa we were met by Woolley, with a felucca and a steam launch lent by the English Commander, and a number of Arabs.[30] It was very exciting to arrive at Beheni where there was the old temple near the water's edge.[31] The camp and the wonderful mound of tombs were at the

27. As Lizzie and her party proceeded by boat south from Luxor to Aswan, one of the small towns along the Nile was Esna. There is an important temple to the god Khnum, the goat-headed local deity (Karl Baedeker, *Egypt and the Sudan* [Leipzig: Karl Baedeker, 1908], 330).

28. Hannah was Lizzie's personal maid; Thomas was Eck's driver and manservant.

29. The village of Shellal was the terminus point for the railway coming to Aswan and also the beginning point for the ferry trip up the Nile to the Second Cataract and Wadi Halfa. When the party reached Halfa they were 802 miles from Cairo (Karl Baedeker, *Egypt and the Sudan* [Leipzig: Karl Baedeker, 1908], 357).

30. "On the east bank of the Nile, 802 miles from Cairo, the town of Wady Halfa marks the site of a part of the district called Buhen. . . . On the western bank of the river . . . are the remains of a temple built by Ustertsen I. . . . Further to the south are fine remains of the temple built by Thothmes II and Thothmes III" (E. A. Wallis Budge, *The Nile: Notes for Travellers in Egypt and in the Egyptian Sudan* [London: Thomas Cook and Son, 1910], 746).

31. On the west bank of the Nile, opposite Wadi Halfa was the ancient town of Beheni. "The South Temple was built by Thutmosis III and dedicated to Horus of Beheni. . . . The admirable mural reliefs, many of which retain their colouring, represent the Pharaoh in presence of the gods. Besides the temples lie the ruins of the ancient town" (Karl Baedeker, *Egypt and the Sudan* [Leipzig: Karl Baedeker, 1908], 402).

top of a high hill of copper coloured sand. Forty Arabs more met us there with their two Sheikhs and Venturi the Italian steward, and Milehan the young English architect who was interested in the ancient Coptic churches. Climbing up the hill you saw the three domes of the camp dazzling white against the deep blue sky and rising out of the red gold sand—from them flew the flags of England and America and in the middle the silver asp of Nubia. How proud and happy Eck was! And how he enjoyed the congenial society of the men and all the things they had to show him. They had all moved into tents except Venturi, who slept in a tomb nearby, the ante-chamber of which was lined with beautiful amethyst coloured rock. The Arab workmen lived at the foot of the hill by the river, and it was the most silent place at night that I have ever seen, not the sounds of a bird or beast, and from the moment the sun went down, not an insect. One morning they showed us the tracks in the sand just behind the camp wall where a caravan had passed in the night—the camels making no sound with their soft-padded feet. Each of us had a little house of our own, or rather a thick-walled cell with a doorway and narrow window with a green blind over each and opening into a little courtyard of its own. The furniture consisted of an iron cot and 2 boxes for washstand and bureau and every morning an Arab brought a big pail of water and filled our tub, in fact, his entire day was spent in bringing up water on a pole in the Venetian way. The Englishman very characteristically had made several little flower beds inside the wall of the camp, and one morning we were too amused to see the whole group of men bending over a tiny dwarfed flower, which they said was the first time the "giant convolvulus" had bloomed. We had an English breakfast of coffee, bacon and eggs, broiled fish, etc. in a room enclosed with green mosquito net. By mid-day, the heat was so intense that we had lunch consisting of a huge mound of rice, or spaghetti with grated cheese and Swedish butter, under the heavy adobe dome of the darkened central building, but by evening when the cool darkness came, we had a most picturesque dinner outside with coloured lanterns hung around and candles in glass shades upon which tall stands, arranged by Venturi, but Dr. MacIver was the wonderful housekeeper. Bean soup, fish croquettes and pigeon pie, all made on a tiny charcoal fire by two dignified Arabs. After dinner it was sometimes so cool that we sat outside in deck chairs covered with shawls and rugs and watched to see the Southern-cross rise. One evening we even had fruit water-ice with ice brought from the Atbara.[32] It was very interesting to see MacIver pay off the men. One evening he sat with his big account book open on the wall and a shaded candle, and standing by him a tall dignified Arab Sheikh and huddled outside seventy or eighty men. As each one's name was called he came up and it was told how much he worked and how much extra backshish was due him for finding special treasures. He was asked if he were satisfied, and in a few gruff words told if he wanted any of the money or wished the sheikh to send it to his family. One evening we enjoyed dining with Captain Poole, head of the English transportation service at Wady Halfa, whose house had many European comforts, which we appreciated fully. The most exciting was the dinner given especially to Emily by the young Governor, Captain Bassett, or Bimbashi, as he was called at the Muhdaria.[33] We went down the river in a felucca, and were received by quite a party of English Officers, some of whom had just come down from Khartoum, and had not seen a white woman for months. When Emily had talked to several a little while, others would come up and say piteously, "Now it's our turn." Dinner was preceded by a tray of cocktails made of champagne and seltzer which they called "Khartoum corpse revivers," the dinner was wonderful in many courses, each with its special wine, and the great hall was hung with flags, many with stories, among them, Kitchener's own flag. It was quite a barbaric looking hall, with spears and javelins and assegais hung

32. The railway junction into the Sudan was at Atbara. It was the point of divergence of the Nile and Red Sea Railway. Because of its importance it would have had amenities, including ice (ibid., 409).

33. Capt. John R. Bassett maintained a lifelong relationship with Emily Sinkler Roosevelt. In the 1950s his stepson Guy Burgess (1911–1963) visited Emily at her South Carolina plantation, Gippy. Burgess, who was a communist spy (of course, unknown to Emily), was given a full-fledged tour of the Charleston area by Emily's niece, Emily Fishburne Whaley. British-born Burgess worked for the BBC, British Intelligence, and the British Foreign Office before serving as second secretary with Kim Philby, first secretary at the British Embassy, in Washington, D.C. ("Guy Burgess, British Intelligence Operative, Spy for the Soviet Union, 1930s–1940s," *The Cold War, 1945–1991*, 3 vols., ed. Benjamin Frankel [Detroit: Gale Research, 1992], reproduced in *Biography Resource Center* [Farmington Hills: Gale Group, 2004]. Available from http://galenet.galegroup.com/servlet/BioRC [accessed June 27, 2005]).

about, dozens and dozens of servants and many dogs eating the crumbs under our feet. But opening out of it was a real English sitting-room, with chintz covered sofas and easy chairs, and big bowls of flowers, which a stalwart young English officer was proud of arranging, saying, of course, all Oxford men knew how to arrange flowers and were accustomed to it. At last I insisted that we must go down to the steamer waiting for us, as we were to sail that night for Shellal, and Dr. MacIver's party, including Eck and Gordon were going back up the river to Buhen. We walked through the gardens of the Muhdaria under the great white oleanders whose blossoms shone like silver in the splashes of moonlight; there were fountains that trickled and vines whose fragrant blossoms fell upon us in that garden and the deep silent Nile flowing by on its mysterious way. The story of how our boat was delayed in getting off until after midnight must remain untold. Going down the river the water had fallen so rapidly that the Arabs were planting water-melon and cucumber seeds in the rich, black, shiny stretches of mud. We then returned to the comfortable hotel of Aswan and waited for Dr. Gordon and Eck to come.[34] They had stayed at another and rougher camp, and visited the old Roman Fort on the river. Eck was more pleased than by anything at finding one morning by

34. Aswan was the southern boundary of Egypt and was known as a health resort in Lizzie's day. "Though a brazen furnace in summer, Assouan can hardly be surpassed as a health resort in winter. Surrounded by desert, the air is dry, yet the usual penalty, dust, is absent. The days are warm and brilliantly sunny, but seldom unpleasantly hot during the winter months." The principle attraction was the new dam. "It is at the upper end of the cataract, at Shellal, about six miles by rail south of Assouan. This work completed in 1902 was four years in the building, and has had a tremendous effect on the prosperity of Egypt. . . . In winter when the river is high some of the water is held back and the reservoir gradually filled. At low Nile, in the spring and summer, when Egypt has hardly enough water to save herself from absolute drought, the sluices are opened and the supply augmented, until, as the river begins to rise for the next flood, the reservoir is empty" (A. O. Lamplough, *Egypt and How to See It* [New York: Doubleday, Page, 1907], 107–8). Aswan was the first town in Egypt north of the actual frontier. It is considered to be in southern Upper Egypt and is noted for many historic sites including major Greco-Roman temples such as Philae, Kom Ombo, Edfu, and Esna. Lizzie and her contemporaries referred to the town and area as Assouan, or Assuan. Today it is known as Aswan (John Baines and Jaromir Malek, *Atlas of Ancient Egypt* [New York: Facts on File, 1980], 70, 71).

the tracks in the sand of his little hut that a small fox had visited him in the night. He often thought of that little fox, and another animal he loved to remember was a little lilac monkey in the garden at Assonan [Assouan] who every time he went there came and picked out the threads of the hem of his white trousers with its tiny claws to look for nuts, which he took care to provide. In that garden also lived a gigantic stork, who strutted angrily and defiantly about the paths, going ahead of anyone and followed by a smaller beautiful creature, some kind of blue crane with a red bill.

While we were in Cairo we had the pleasure of seeing the opera of *Aida* in the opera house for which it was written by Verdi. The jewels were all real and copied from the old ones found in the tombs, for the Khedive squandered money lavishly when entertaining the Empress, and the soldiers were of course, real Soudanese. There were two boxes screened by thick gauze for the harem ladies.

The heat at Aswan while we were waiting for the train to take us down to Cairo was something unspeakable as it was really too late in the season for us to have stayed and the queer black sullen-looking rocks seemed to increase it. I remember one night sitting out on a little balcony out of my room, clad in my thinnest nightgown, and first there came floating by a boatload of Germans, who tried to think they were on the Rhine, singing Volkslieder. Then to my surprise a man in evening clothes strolled about, playing on the Scotch bag-pipes a very romantic and melancholy air, which seemed to affect Dr. Gordon so much that he went off and sat dismally on one of the sullen black rocks, and finally a boat full of Greeks who had been working at the great dam, came by singing their native songs.

It was too late in the season to go down from Aswan by boat, so we took a train and passed through a great sandstorm.[35] The blue glasses were all down and through them the affect was curious like a snow storm or blizzard. The Arabs long garments almost whipped off them and the palm

---

35. As Lizzie noted, it was too late in the season to take one of Cook's Nile steamers, and so they had to take the less comfortable train. "At Luxor the line changes to narrow gauge, but the same tradition of comfort is maintained in the trains. The windows are fitted with smoked glass to counteract the glare, and a luncheon-car is attached to the train. The journey to Assouan takes six and a half hours" (A. O. Lamplough, *Egypt and How to See It* [New York: Doubleday, Page, 1907], 98).

trees bent double by a furious storm. We had a wonderful blessing, however, after the terrible heat of the train hermetically sealed from the sandstorm, in a cool change coming when we got to a junction were the sleepers were put on, and to our joy they gave us a special car for our party of nine or ten. Each one having a compartment and bed with linen sheets. We stayed at the Gezireh Palace hotel this time in Cairo, or rather on the other side of the Nile and it was a delightful experience.[36] The gardens were so big and beautiful and the rooms magnificent. This was the palace where the Khedive Ismail entertained the Empress Eugenie at the time of the Suez Canal, and the gorgeous furnishing of the rooms was like an Arabian Nights' dream.[37] Our drawing room was so large that it was quite a walk to go from one end of it to the other, and it hung directly over the Nile. But my bath-room, which was almost as large, was the most interesting of all, as it contained a huge bath-tub of solid silver, with the Empress Eugenie's Monogram handsomely embossed on it. When I heard that after her visit was over, and the Khedive Ismail took up his abode there, that he sometimes drowned his wives in it, I did not enjoy my bath so much. One night before going to bed, Eckley came and told me that he saw a strange thing. His room, although smaller than mine, had the walls covered with velvet hangings, and on accidentally moving one, he

36. Khedive Ismail Pasha built many grand palaces in Cairo, one of which was the Ghezireh Palace on the left bank of the Nile, opposite Boulak (J. A. McCoan, *Egypt* [New York: Peter Fenelon Collier, 1898], 56).

37. "The Ghezireh Palace Hotel in the former viceregal palace is a huge and sumptuously fitted up house with accommodations for 350 guests, electric lights, lifts, ball room and theatre, large gardens, telegraph office, lawn-tennis courts, and casino." Ferdinand de Lesseps began to dream about the Suez Canal as early as 1836. The canal was begun in 1859 with British funding. There were twenty-five thousand workmen on the project. On March 18, 1869, the canal was completed at a cost of 19 million pounds sterling (Karl Baedeker, *Egypt and the Sudan* [Leipzig: Karl Baedeker, 1908], 177). Khedive Ismail had been schooled in France, so it was not surprising that he invited Empress Eugenie of France to the elaborate dedicatory ceremonies, which began on November 17, 1869. The opera *Aida* was written by Giuseppe Verdi for the canal opening. Today's Cairo Marriot Hotel is the same Ghezireh Palace Hotel built as a palace for Empress Eugenie. The entire extravagant and lavish entertainment and construction projects for the celebration helped bankrupt the Egyptian government (*Egypt Eyewitness Travel Guide* [London: Dorling Kindersley, 2001], 60–61).

discovered a locked door, and through the keyhole a light shining. There were no signs of this door in the anteroom on the other side—so we rang for the watchman, who seemed quite annoyed, as he confessed there was a secret staircase between the walls, which had formerly been used to carry up things from boats on the river to a kitchen—or, we were told by some one else, to throw any one down they wanted to get rid of, as the steps led into the river. Every morning early while we were staying at the Gezireh, an English Captain rode by Emily's window, and sent up his Arab sayce with a message or note or flowers. All sorts of interesting things came to my mind—such as the mysterious trick shown by an Indian juggler who came one day to perform in front of a hotel in the brilliant sunshine on the broad gravel road, with not a bush or tree near, and only a small group looking on. He had a large oval basket, with a cover, on the ground, which he kicked over, and took off the lid to show us it was empty. After a while when he was showing other tricks, we noticed that the basket was shaking slightly. He took off the lid, and there was a large, black, fat man, wedged inside so tight that he could hardly get out. It was really quite incomprehensible. One day Sophy invited us to dine at the Mena House,[38] and it is a lovely evening to remember. We walked first to see the great pyramids and the sphinx in the sunset, and back to the hotel in the dusk, where we had a very entertaining dinner and then drove back to Cairo in a large open barouche in the moonlight.[39] Gordon, MacIver and Woolley were all with

38. Mena House Hotel, still in operation today, was located near the pyramids of Gizeh and was an extensive establishment and famous as a health resort. "With 180 rooms, swimming and other baths, stables, riding track, carriages, sand carts, dog carts, and cycles for hire, lawn tennis courts, a library of 600 English books . . . [it] is recommended for invalids" (Karl Baedeker, *Egypt and the Sudan* [Leipzig: Karl Baedeker, 1908], 31).

39. "The best way to see the Pyramids is to hire a donkey at Cairo in the cool of the evening, and ride to the Mena House Hotel, at the foot of the Pyramids, to sleep. By this means the Pyramid can be climbed in comfort and comparative privacy early the next morning before the usual horde of tourists arrive from Cairo." The pyramids were built in the Fourth Dynasty, of limestone from the Mokattam quarries and cased with polished granite slabs. Since the height is over 451 feet, there was the obvious question of how a lady in a long skirt would climb up this immense mass. "Two or three Arabs practically haul the visitor up to the top and only a couple of halts are as a rule allowed the breathless climber. . . . The summit

us, and Emily sang and others repeated poetry, and the scent of the orange blossoms floated to us over the walls of the Harem gardens that we drove by. After a while we took a steamer from Alexandria back to Naples leaving Sophy to our sorrow with her friends near Cairo. Then Gordon sailed back to America from Naples, and Woolley remained with us, showing us some wonderful places, as he had done a good deal of excavating in Italy. Eck came very near buying the Castle of Baiea, which was for sale for a tiny price, and a most fascinating place on a point of land, with its own port and lighthouse and chapel and two drawbridges and moats, and the most enchanting terraces. But as it would have been necessary to build a great elevator and rebuild the dwelling rooms, and as, unfortunately, there are only twelve months in the year, so there would have been no time for us ever to stay there, and that beautiful dreamland had to be abandoned. We stopped at a little inn for lunch where Woolley knew the people, and they gave us a dish of six kinds of fish, one being cuttle fish, and their own wine and oranges.

One afternoon we drove down to Pozznoli for tea at the most fascinating restaurant under an arbour of wisteria, whose blossoms carpeted the floor and scented the air, and the landlady handed us cake made of honey and almonds which she said they always presented their guests with at Easter. On our way from Naples to Rome we stopped over at Teano to see the picturesque country and the beautiful old dilapidated palace belonging to a very impoverished prince where Woolley had stayed for sometime while doing archaeological work near by. Emily had quite an amusing little episode with the young prince, who had no idea of being polite to us until he saw her, and then was most pressing in his attentions. His father was away, and Woolley disliked the young one very much.

We had an enchanting visit to Rome and then to Perugia and Assisi, which it would be tiresome to try to describe, but I must speak of the tombs of the Volumni, not long ago discovered between those places—with the curious statutes and sarcophagi, each in their little underground chambers, and sticking out of the wall the fierce head of a serpent—the guardian of the tombs.

---

reached, a magnificent view may be enjoyed during the regulation half hours rest (E. A. Reynolds-Ball, *Cairo of To-Day: A Practical Guide to Cairo and its Environs* [London: Adam and Charles Black, 1899], 120–24).

CHAPTER SEVEN

From Paris to Istanbul on the Orient Express, 1910

Lizzie and her party traveled in 1910 on the famed Orient Express from Paris to Istanbul. The Orient Express, the "pearl of the Orient," was the epitome of great trains with exquisite wood paneling, fine china, immaculate linens, and Lalique crystal. Its first run was in 1883 from Gare de l'Est in Paris. By 1910 its fame had spread. On this trip Lizzie was in the company of her young nieces Anne Wickham Sinkler and Laura Stevens. Family legend had it that Anne had fallen in love with a young country doctor, William Kershaw Fishburne. Anne's mother, Anne Wickham Porcher Sinkler, did not approve of the young, impoverished doctor and so arranged with her sister-in-law that Anne be taken out of the country for five months, hoping to distract her attentions. The grand plan did not work. It is said that Anne returned to the United States and fell off the train at Branchville, South Carolina, into the arms of Kershaw Fishburne. They were married on April 14, 1910.

Turkey in 1910 was an exotic, Muslim country with close ties to Germany. Lizzie traveled in style. The foursome stayed in the fashionable suburb of Pera. It was in this more modern setting that the European governments built their new embassies and consulates. Pera Galata was the district to the north, across the Golden Horn from the old city of Constantinople. The Pera Palace Hotel had been constructed by the Orient Express line in 1892 expressly to host visitors arriving on the Orient Express train from Paris and Venice. The hotel had exquisite views over the Golden Horn and was a stately six stories. The Golden Horn was a small gulf separating the ancient city of Constantinople from suburbs to the north. Two small rivers fed this gulf, one of which, the Kagithane, was nicknamed the Sweet Waters of Europe. The term "Golden" was appropriate because of the glow from the gardens and palaces of the sultans and great Ottoman families who resided along the banks of this small gulf. The Pera Palace overlooked this gulf. Its public rooms were deeply carpeted in Persian rugs. Lizzie's party had spacious rooms in this grand old hotel.

Lizzie made good use of her extensive and well placed connections. Ambassador John G. A. Leishman was a native of Pittsburgh and a wealthy industrialist. He was a friend of Eck and Lizzie, and made arrangements for them to see the jewels in the Sultan's treasury, located in the Imperial Treasury in the Third Court of the Topkapi Sarayi. Ambassador Leishman had purchased Palazzo Corpi, a magnificent building which was to become the U. S. embassy in 1907.

Another notable acquaintance was Herman V. Hilprecht, one of the outstanding Assyriologists. Hilprecht lived between his native Germany and the United States. He was an important figure in the expansion of Semitic studies in the United States to include Akkadian and Sumerian, the languages of ancient Mesopotamia. Lizzie and Eck knew Hilprecht because he was a lecturer at the University of Pennsylvania in 1886. He had begun as a lecturer in Egyptology but assumed a professorship of Assyriology and comparative Semitic philology. He had done extensive excavations at Nippur, a Sumerian city that had been occupied for three millennia.[1] Dr. Hilprecht shepherded Lizzie's party through the museum in the several parts of the Sultan's former seraglio (harem palace). The sultans had moved in 1853 from the seraglio, called the Topkapi Palace, to a modern palace on the Bosphorus, called the Dolmabahce Palace. The Museum of Oriental Antiquities, which Lizzie's party visited, housed the antiquities and treasures from all over Anatolia and the Middle Eastern dominions of the Ottoman Empire including ancient Mesopotamia. It was part of the Topkapi complex, the original palace of the Sultans. Lizzie's party also visited the Dolmabahce Palace during their stay at the small town of Tarabya on the Bosphorus. Lizzie, Carrie, Eck, Laura, and Anne had the pleasure of seeing Turkey at a time when it still held much of the flavor of the old East.

1. Benjamin R. Foster, "Herman Vollrath Hilprecht," in *American National Biography*, ed. John A. Garraty and Mark C. Carnes, 10 vols. (New York: Oxford University Press, 1999), 10: 825–27.

This world is all a fleeting show
for mans illusion Given
The smiles of Joy the tears of woe
Deceitful shine deceitful flow
Theres nothing true but Heaven

And false the light on glorys plume
As fading lines of even
And love and Hope and beauties bloom
Are blessings gathered for the tomb
Theres nothing bright but Heaven

Poor wanderers of a stormy day
From wave to wave we're driven
And fancy's flash and reasons ray
Save but to light our troubeled way
Theres nothing calm but Heaven
                          Thomas moore

"There's Nothing Calm but Heaven," drawing by E. A. Coxe

March 10

Dearest Wharton —

It is too queer
to be here and more oriental
& barbaric than anything
you can imagine — although
they call it a modern town &
a "luxurious" hotel etc. — & really
are building very handsome
government buildings. The
Governor's Palace — built on the
site of Gordon's — is very fine &
in the midst of a tropical garden.
There is the Gordon Memorial —
College — & a large hospital &
English & Egyptian barracks
all built on the high bank —

Stationery from Grand Hotel Khartoum, Sudan (above), and SS Rameses the
Great, *Luxor (facing page), 1905*

S.S. "RAMESES THE GREAT,"

Luxor

March 22 1905

Dearest Anne & Charlie

The girls have arrived!
and are well & safe and
looking splendidly!

This morning at 8.30
Carry, Eck & I with a carriage
4 donkeys, 4 donkey boys
& 2 dragomen went to
the station to meet them —
there we found Cook had sent
their finest dragoman also
as a telegram had arrived
"Send special man to meet
2 young ladies Sinkler"

A felucca on the Nile, 1905; courtesy of the University of Pennsylvania Museum

Anne Sinkler and Emily Sinkler arriving at the train station in Luxor, Egypt, 1905; courtesy of the University of Pennsylvania Museum

Lizzie's nieces in the streets of Cairo, 1905

Above and top facing: Anne Sinkler and Emily Sinkler visit the Great Sphinx and the pyramids, Egypt, 1905

Arriving in Alexandria, Egypt, for the trip to Nubia, 1909

The camp at Buhen, Nubia, 1909

Buhen, Nubia, 1909: Eckley B. Coxe, Jr. (seated center); C. Leonard Woolley, (far right); David Randall-MacIver (standing, third from right); Elizabeth Sinkler Coxe (seated, second from left); and Caroline S. Sinkler (seated, second from right); both photographs courtesy of the University of Pennsylvania Museum

Tent and soldier at Buhen, 1909

Women and children with baskets, Nubia, 1909; both photographs courtesy of the University of Pennsylvania Museum

Eckley B. Coxe, Jr., with statuette of Merer in Buhen, Nubia, 1909; courtesy of the University of Pennsylvania Museum

Statue of the scribe Ahmose, Buhen, 1909; courtesy of the University of Pennsylvania Museum

Constantinople, including (above) the wall, (below) the bridge at Galata, and (next page) Santa Sophia, 1910, from Lizzie's photo album

The Acropolis at Athens (above and below)

The harbor at Smyrna, 1910

Lizzie and her niece Emily Sinkler, undated, from Lizzie's photo album

Lizzie's nieces: (below) Emily Sinkler and Elizabeth Stevens in Florence; (left) Emily Sinkler and Elizabeth Stevens in Egypt. Undated, from Lizzie's photograph album

Emily Sinkler and Elizabeth Stevens at St. Marks, Venice

Although many Turks replaced their traditional, bright-colored garb with European clothing, the country was a polyglot of different nationalities and cultures, including Greeks, Jews, Armenians, Serbs, and Turks. Much of this special ambience was to disappear after World War I with the reforms of Mustafa Kemal Ataturk, who came to power in 1923 with the abolition of the Sultanate. Ataturk sought to modernize Turkey. He abolished the fez and abandoned the Arabic alphabet, replacing it with the Latin equivalent. He embarked on ambitious plans for political and economic modernization. Thus the Turkey that Lizzie and her small party enjoyed was unique, an amalgam of the cultures of Greece, Rome, and Persia, and a composite of the antiquities from Byzantium, Constantinople, and Istanbul. After a lengthy stay in Istanbul, the travelers went by steamer through the Sea of Marmara and spent several days in Smyrna and Athens before returning through Switzerland and Trento on their homeward trek to the United States. Following is Lizzie's journal entry.

> One of our most delightful trips was to Constantinople. It began by sailing from New York on the *Kaiserin Auguste Victoria*[2] with Anne and Laura, besides Eck, Carrie and myself. This was the most luxurious ship we were ever on. There were lifts taking you from deck to deck, delightful saloons to read and write, and decks to walk and sit. And a "Ritz Carlton" tea room with lattices of ivy and blooming plants and lovely country scenes in panels, and a scarlet clad Hungarian orchestra, etc. Then there was a gymnasium where you could trot on a camel or donkey as you like and do every kind of stunt. In fact there was everything to make you forget you were on the water.
>
> We arrived at Plymouth on a beautiful moonlight night when the search-lights outvied the moon in throwing their great bars of light across the harbour, and there came out on a tender Ella and Wharton who spent the night with us on board and crossed to Cherbourg whence we went to Paris by rail. While waiting for the ladder to be put down, Wharton

2. When the SS *Kaiserin Auguste Victoria* was launched by the Hamburg-Amerika line in 1905, it was the largest ship in the world at 705 feet in length and at 24,581 gross tons in weight. The ship and its crew of 593 accommodated 652 first-class passengers, 286 second-class passengers, 216 third-class passengers, and 1,842 persons in steerage. Pictures of the interior show that Lizzie was apt in characterizing it as elegant and luxurious.

handed up on a long pole, the most enchanting basket of English flowers I ever saw. Wall flowers, primroses, iris, daffodils—every lovely thing.

We stopped in Paris together at Maurice's for a week or two—making delightful little excursions and having a very happy time, and then they went to the Gare d'Este and saw us off on the Oriental Express on which we had a most interesting trip. Our first stop was at Vienna where we spent two days seeing all the sights under the escort of Ober Leftenant Nansi Teuber, who changed his gorgeous uniforms three or four times a day, and took us out to see his mother and Charlotte's children at their villa.

As this was a great race day and all the equipages engaged, he had to borrow horses from his regiment for two Victorias, and he and Anne and I sat together in one, I acting as interpreter as best I might for a gay little flirtation between them.

Our next stop was at Buda Pesth, that beautiful city on two sides of the Danube. There, too, we spent two days, driving about and listening to music. The great swirling notes of the zimbals seemed to fill the air all night with its curious throbbing emotional sounds. At the Parliament house there we were much interested in seeing a picture by Charles Young that we heard they had bought.

Then we pursued our way past Bucharest, Belgrade and Sofia, and at last reached Constantinople in a cold, dismal rain. The last twenty miles or more, there was a Turkish sentinel with his rifle ready every quarter of a mile along the track, looking so miserable that the girls threw out chocolate to them whenever they could. The night before our big Alsatian conductor told us that we would cross the border after midnight and must be prepared to see two Turkish officers, one young and one old, come into our rooms and search everything. This was a grand great excitement to the girls, who prepared by tying their hair up in becoming little bows of pink ribbon, and declared that they would not dream of going to sleep, but begged me to leave the door open between our compartments. I was awakened later on by a stifled little scream, and saw the two Turks in fezzes and gorgeous uniforms come in, preceded by our big Alsatian and Laura's face of terror, her cheeks scarlet, and her big black eyes staring with fright. They poked into all our bags, and under our pillows, and afterwards we missed our prayer books and all Eck's round tickets back to Paris—for which, however, Cook refunded part.

At the station in Constantinople, kind Dr. Hilprecht met us, and helped us through the trials of the suspicious Custom House, and then guided us to the Pera Palace Hotel where he had engaged our rooms. It was on a high eminence and the views from our windows were beautiful and interesting. Our nights were very wakeful with the barking of the gangs of dogs, the tapping of the watchman's metal tipped stick on the pavement, which must have been a great help to all miscreants, giving them plenty of time to get away.[3] Then there was the curious music of the Turks, who seemed to serenade their fair ladies all night with some whining caterwauling songs and an instrument of the same nasal tone. Of course, the barking and the quarreling of the gangs of dogs was the most exciting noise of all. As they were very fierce and dangerous I was quite uneasy at Eck's going out in his pajamas to give them any biscuits and sandwiches he could collect.[4]

3. "Pera is a mongrel city, set on a height and streaming blatantly to Galata; a city of tall, discolored houses not unlike the houses of Naples; of embassies and churches; of glaring shops and cafes glittering with plate-glass, through which crafty, impudent eyes are forever staring out upon the passers-by; of noisy, unattractive hotels and wizen gardens, where bands play at stated hours, and pretentious, painted women from second rate European music halls posture and squall under the light of electric lamps. There is no rest, no peace in Pera. There seems to be no discipline. . . . They have a special breed of cars in Pera. Bicyclists are allowed to use motor sirens to clear the way before them. . . . Pera has all that is odious of the Levant: impudence, ostentation, slyness, indelicacy, uproar, a glittering commonness. . . . Stamboul is harmonious, is very beautiful. Romance seems brooding over it, trailing lights and shadows to clothe it with flame and with darkness. It holds you, it entices you. It sheds upon you a sense of mystery" (Robert Hichens, *The Near East, Dalmatia, Greece, and Constantinople* [New York: Century, 1913], 188–92).

4. "To omit all reference to the dogs of a city which has been styled a 'dog-kennel' is impossible. . . . They are one of the prominent features in the street-scenery of the city. . . . Tawny in colour, with a furry coat, bushy tail, and pointed ears, they betray their relationship to the wolf and the fox. . . . To some extent they act also as watchmen, making night hideous with their barking. . . . The different quarters of Constantinople are respectively the special domains of different companies of dogs, who guard their boundaries as jealously and fiercely as any frontiers between rival nations" (Alexander Van Millingen and Warwick Goble, *Constantinople* [London: A & C Black, 1906], 212–13).

Constantinople is full of intensely interesting things. Then there is the open square called the "Hippodrome" with the wonderful serpent pillar and obelisk and fountain.[5] And then most wonderful of all are the beautiful mosques—. Santa Sophia is superb with its wonderful pillars, no two alike.[6] One they showed us had a crimson stain high up, where they said Mohamet placed his hand when he rode in over the bodies of the thousands of Christians who lay massacred in heaps on the floor. Then there was the old mosaic mosque covered with pictures of Christian saints and symbols, which the Mohametans have tried to whitewash or tear out, but some of them still shine out clearly.[7] Another mosque lined with the most exquisite old tiles, was very beautiful. I think it is in the court of this mosque that the tomb of the Sultan who married a beautiful Christian

5. Today the tree-shaded park before the Blue Mosque is on the site of the ancient Roman Hippodrome. The race track was built in 198 c.e. by the Emperor Septimius Severus and expanded by Emperor Constantine in 330. It was the scene of chariot races between the sociopolitical factions of Constantinople, as well as for acclaiming victories. It fell into ruins and by 1609 served as a quarry for the construction of the Blue Mosque. The Egyptian Obelisk was first erected in Egypt by Pharaoh Tutmosis III (sixteenth century b.c.e.) and stood 195 feet tall. It broke apart while being unloaded at Constantinople, and only the top third was mounted by Theodosius the Great in the Hippodrome in 390. The Serpent Column is a twisting shaft of three entwined snakes. Constantine the Great had it brought from the Temple of Apollo at Delphi as it celebrated the victory of the Greek city-states over the Persians at Platea in 479 b.c.e. (*Istanbul* [New York: Alfred A. Knopf, 1998], 176–77).

6. Haghia Sophia was built in five years (532–37 c.e.) by the Emperor Justinian. It is dedicated to "devine wisdom" an attribute of Christ. Justinian called for provincial governors all over the Byzantine Empire to send the most beautiful parts of ancient monuments found in their regions for incorporation. Thus columns and ornaments from pagan temples including Ephesus, Athens, Delphi, Delos, and Egypt were sent, and no two columns are alike. Each of the capitals of the columns is unique, but all are based on acanthus-leaf and palm-foliage motifs (ibid., 74, 143).

7. This is undoubtedly the Church of St. Savior-in-Chora, today the Kariye Cami'i , a Muslim mosque. Built just outside the Constantinian walls and hence in the country, this building dates from 1077. There has been a church on this site since about 413, when Constantinople did not extend beyond the walls of Constantine and this place was outside the city limits. It has superb and numerous Byzantine mosaics and frescoes (ibid., 234).

named Roxana is, and in a separate little domed building is her tomb covered with a magnificent velvet pall embroidered in precious stones. You are not obliged to put on slippers to enter her abode, but you have to for his as in all mosques.[8]

Of course, we spent an afternoon in a caique on the sweet waters of Europe and Asia, which, however, is a poor imitation of an evening in a gondola at Venice[9] with the lovely music of guitars and Italian songs, and the cupolas and domes against the sky.[10] We spent a day or two most

8. Roxelana, literally the Russian, became the wife of the famous sixteenth-century sultan, Suleyman I. The Suleymaniye Mosque was an imposing mosque complex designed and built by the famous architect Sinan. It stands on a broad platform on the summit of the third hill. The dome is 86 feet in diameter and 156 feet in height. Begun in 1550 it was completed in 1557, and the complex included the tombs of both Suleyman and Roxelana. The tiles, as mentioned by Lizzie, depict flowers and foliage and are fired in turquoise, sapphire, and red on a pure white ground, while the walls and pillars were veneered with colored marbles. In addition the stained-glass windows are of rich color and beautiful design. The tomb of Roxelana is covered with blue and white tiles while the dome is elaborately decorated with arabesques (*Handbook for Travellers in Constantinople, Brusa, and the Troad with Maps and Plans* [London: John Murray, 1900], 61).

9. Lizzie and her nieces Emily Sinkler and Elizabeth Stevens visited Venice on this trip in 1909, and there are wonderful photographs from that trip of the three of them feeding pigeons in St. Mark's Square and enjoying a gondola ride under the Bridge of Sighs.

10. The Golden Horn was a gulf of the Bosphorus that separated old walled Constantinople from its suburbs, including Galata and Pera, where Lizzie and her party were staying. The name Golden Horn is derived from the resemblance of this arm of the Bosporus to the shape of a ram's horn. It is six miles long, and its upper reaches were the favorite relaxation place of the ladies of Constantinople. During the time of Lizzie's visit there was a Friday promenade, which was frequented by Turkist society. Caiques, which were small pointed rowboats, plied these "sweet" waters, so called because the two small rivers that fed the Golden Horn, the Alibey and the Kagithane, were formerly nicknamed the Sweet Waters of Europe. "The swallow-boats are formed of thin planks of beech wood, neatly finished and elaborately carved. The elegance of their construction, the extreme lightness of the wood of which they are composed, and the dexterity of the boatmen, cause them to glide over the smooth surface of the waters with great rapidity. . . . Next to gondolas, they are the easiest and most comfortable of all boats" (*Handbook for Travellers in Constantinople*), 89.

delightfully at Therapia on the Bosphorus where the summer palaces of the Embassies are, and also of the Turkish grandees.[11] The water is covered with their beautiful barges, and all sorts of picturesque shipping, and in the far distance, they point out to you the opening into the Black Sea and the black smoke of warships. We paid a visit to our Ambassador there, Mr. Leishman, for our Ambassadors to Turkey always seem to have German-Jew names. He was very proud in having succeeded in getting Congress to purchase a palace in Pera for the U.S. Embassy—the first that we own in any country. Mrs. Leishman was a very striking looking woman with scarlet hair and a white lace dress. He got us a permission to visit the Sultan's Treasury, which was quite an important and interesting ceremony. We were accompanied by a fierce looking kavass with a scimitar, and as a matter of courtesy the English embassy had been offered the privilege of sending some visitors with us. We were taken to one of the Sultan's beautiful white marble palaces on the Bosphorous and trays of coffee and rose -leaf preserves handed, with a bowl of rose water and gold fringed napkins.[12] Then a guard of soldiers took us to the Treasury.

11. Therapia, or Tarabya, is a lovely village on the European shore of the Bosphorus that became a favorite resort of Greeks, and the affluent of Pera. At Therapia are the official summer palaces of the German, Italian, French, and British ambassadors. Therapia, which means healing, gets its name from the salubrity of the air, for the cool winds blow directly from the Black Sea and temper the heat of summer. "The best time to spend a few days here is in May or June, when, in the soft twilight of a calm evening, one can wander about amongst cypresses and pine trees with the glassy Bosporus spread out beneath" (ibid., 99).

12. The white marble palace referred to was the Dolmabahce Palace, the grand imperial residence of the Sultans on the Bosphorus from 1853 forward. It was built by Sultan Abdul Mejid. Its entire front of 814 feet faces the Bosphorus and is gleaming white marble. The total number of rooms was 285, and obviously from Lizzie's comments, one of them must have been a closely guarded Treasury with crown jewels. "The interior is fitted up in a luxurious manner with large mirrors, crystal chandeliers and candelabra, chimney pieces of malachite and Sevres china, gaudily painted ceilings, and cupolas of stained glass, through which a flood of rich, warm light pours down. . . . The great central hall or throne room is profusely decorated. . . . Adjoining the central hall is the Harem. . . . The gardens of the palace are celebrated for their beauty and are reserved for the use of the ladies of the Harem." The Bosporus extends from its junction with the Sea of Marmora and the Golden Horn to the Black Sea, and divides Europe from Asia. The strait is nineteen

We saw the wonderful jewels: the turbans of all the Sultans for many years, with cockades and stars of magnificent rubies, emeralds and diamonds; boxes and swords all set with the same ropes of pearls and even a throne entirely encrusted with uncut precious stones—, which to my eyes lack the beauty of the cut ones. A Turkish officer of high rank walked around with us, with a very bored and haughty air. When we left a guard of soldiers watched and an old gentleman, evidently of important position, after locking the door affixed an immense clay seal to it.

Dr. Hilprecht took us to the Museum, which I think is partly the old Seraglio with fine large rooms added, and his own rooms were lofty and beautiful, and the tablets he discovered at Nippur shown to great advantage in glass cases. There were some beautiful sculptures and Sarcophagi, and most valuable of all the Sarcophagus of Alexander the Great.[13]

Every one has heard of the porters of Constantinople, but the most wonderful thing was Mrs. Hilprecht telling me that when she ordered an upright piano, she saw to her dismay it coming up the streets of Pera on the back of a single man.[14]

---

miles long and is a succession of lovely woodlands dotted with villages. The word *Bosporus* is a Greek one meaning "Ox-passage" and has its origin in the fable of Io, who was changed into a heifer by Jupiter and swam across these straits (ibid., 93–94).

13. Lizzie and her party were in the Archaeological Museum in the Topkapi Palace, which in 1910 would have been called the Imperial Museum of Antiquities. It was situated on the Seraglio grounds. As a result of the discovery in 1888 in Saida (the Sidon of the Ancients) of twenty-one Hellenic sarcophagi, a new museum was built at the behest of Sultan Abdul-Hamid II and had a distinguished curator, Hamdi Bey. It opened in 1892. Among its treasures was the supposed Alexander the Great sarcophagus. The scenes carved on the marble represent a battle between the Persians and the Greeks as well as lion and stag hunts. The sarcophagus, which is over ten feet long is modeled to represent an elongated Greek temple with its friezes and pediments. The museum also includes a marble head of Alexander the Great copied after the famous original by Lysippus. In 334 B.C.E. Alexander crossed the Hellespont (today's Dardanelles) and freed the Greek city-states from Persian rule (Demetrius Coufopoulos, *A Guide to Constantinople* [London: Adam and Charles Black, 1899], 85–114).

14. The streets of old Istanbul were extremely steep and narrow. In many places they were too narrow for carts and wagons, and so loads were carried by donkeys and by human beings on their backs. These individuals were called "hamals." "In

The old walls of the city and the picturesque round towers, and the beautiful cemeteries with tall, pointed cypresses, where it is said many mysterious love affairs are secretly carried on—how. How can I describe all these without being tiresome.[15]

Then came the most beautiful of all voyages, crossing the sea of Marmora in a little steamer with the deck arranged like an observation car, and we glided through the Isles of Greece and saw Mount Olympus and every other beautiful famous mountain and island, and finally that evening into the beautiful Bay of Smyrna. And it all seemed like a wonderful vision we had been permitted to see. Of course, the heat and mosquitoes at the showy but uncomfortable hotel that night were disillusioning, and next day we were not allowed to go to Ephesus, because they said the brigands were too dangerous, and Dr. Hilprecht had seen the year before the heads of a half dozen of them hung over the city gate. But we had a very interesting morning, driving about the town and seeing the camel bridge, and the great market place where all the caravans from Asia Minor come in. The camels are much larger than the Egyptian ones and we saw a long string of them arriving, tied nose to tail, and the last one has a small bell on his tail, so if he is stolen or strayed they know the string is not complete. Laura insisted on riding a camel, so they mounted her on a perfect giantess of a lady camel, and as soon as she began to lope poor

---

the affairs of residents, hamals occupy an important place. They carry the merchant's goods to and fro. They bring your charcoal, your coal, your wood, your stoves, your piano, your chest of drawers, every heavy piece of your furniture. They will even carry a child in their arms up a hill or to a distant house, as tenderly as any nurse" (Alexander Van Millingen and Warwick Goble, *Constantinople* [London: A & C Black, 1906], 207–8).

15. Land and sea walls encircled old Byzantium. They were completed in 413 C.E. during the reign of Emperor Theodosius II, and at their inception they had over one hundred round towers. Eventually the triple-wall system included a moat that could be flooded. As Lizzie notes, outside these walls were innumerable cemeteries, which were referred to as "fields of the dead." The need for fortifications resulted from the fact that old Byzantium stood as a fulcrum between East and West and was to become a bulwark that "met, and broke, successive stormwaves of Asiatic attack, until in due season a strong Asiatic race forced its way in" (B. Granville Baker, *The Walls of Constantinople* [New York: James Pott, 1910], 17). See illustrations of the old walls and towers throughout this book.

Laura was seized with terror and cried out, "Don't let the baby camel come near her." It was all too funny. We were quite provoked that although it was now June, there were no figs to be had in Smyrna. Next day we went on to Athens, and going through the Corinth Canal, the water was like a pale green emerald, and the banks cut down smoothly like a cheese, but in some places there had been great breaks, and the Captain said that he would never again take such a large ship through it, as the sides almost touched us. Then a few days in Athens at the cool empty marble lined hotel, and then up to Rome, where it was also empty of tourists and consequently comfortable and charming. St. Peters scarcely changes its temperature winter or summer. It was this year, I think that we went to see Charlotte in Trento, that most beautiful town on the border of the Tyrol, with the encircling mountains and beautiful trees. The town itself is beautiful. The palaces are built of pink marble and the streets paved with white marble, and full of wonderful old fountains and statues.[16] Charlotte looked very handsome in white lace and diamond earrings, and Imra in his light blue Austrian uniform and followed by an enormous dog, they showed us everything in the town, from the splendid old Cathedral, with its green tiled roof and curious staircase to the Bishop's palace on the hill, where the Council of Trent was held, but now the barracks for the Austrian Tyrol soldiers. There were almost as many priests as soldiers in town, and they had a procession while we were there, when hundreds of little children carried white lilies, and a little shirt, supposed to have been worn by Christ was carried aloft in a glass case. The next time we stopped at Trento, we saw Charlotte with her little baby,

16. "Trent (630ft.) or Trento, Lat, Tridentum, with 27,100 inhabitants, the wealthiest town in S. Tyrol, owed its early importance to its position at the junction of the road leading from Venice through the Val Sugana to the Brenner road. It has belonged to Austria since 1814, but with its numerous towers, palaces, and broad streets, still presents all the characteristics of an important Italian town." Important places to visit include the Piazza Dante with its lofty monument to Dante by Zocchi (1896); the Palazza Municipale, containing the Museo Comunale; and the church of Santa Maria Maggiore, which contains a picture from 1563 with portraits of the members of the Council of Trent (1545–63); the Cathedral or Duomo, with wonderful frescoes; and the imposing Castello del Buon Consiglio, erected in 1474 as the residence of the bishops (Karl Baedeker, *Northern Italy* [Leipzig: Karl Baedeker, 1913], 23–24).

little Emerica, only a few weeks old. The little soul was wrapped in swad-
dling clothes and tied up in an embroidered pique pillow case with an
immense bow of pink ribbon. From there we went on to Botsen, to
Cortina in the Dolomites which was fascinating—but I fear that I am
using my adjectives until they are threadbare. Back of the hotel is a
hemlock wood and lovely meadows, where one day I gathered twenty-four
varieties of wild flowers. We had five little rooms with balconies looking
over these flowerspangled meadows.

Postscript

Lizzie and Eck died only three years apart, both at their "dear" home at Windy Hill. The lovely house is still there, carefully tended by Philip Brinton Young.

Eckley Brinton Coxe Jr. died at the age of forty-four, on September 21, 1916, of Addison's disease, a complication of tuberculosis. His pallbearers included his father's old friend John Cadwalader; his uncle Wharton Sinkler; and his first cousin Seaman Deas Sinkler (1879–1927). His friend and colleague Dr. George E. Gordon, curator of the University Museum, was also a pallbearer. He was buried in Woodlands Cemetery. He bequeathed $500,000 to the museum of the University of Pennsylvania, exclusively for the use of the Egyptian section, to aid in explorations and to defray the expenses of transportation and publications. There was over $870,000 in total bequests, with other beneficiaries including the Children's Hospital, an endowment of $100,000 to the University of Pennsylvania to increase professors' salaries, and a small amount of $10,000 to provide Christmas presents each year for children in the Children's Hospital.

The *Public Ledger* of September 22, 1916, reported that the board of the Children's Hospital adopted this resolution: "Mr. Coxe was elected to the board of managers on April 6, 1900 and from that day to this has been to an unusual degree faithful and devoted to its interests. Gifted with a heart brimful of sympathy for all forms of suffering and with the means to do good abundantly to those who were in need, his generosity knew no bounds and with his gifts went also the warmest solicitude for the beneficiaries. His modest, unobtrusive ways covered but did not conceal a force of character in which determination to be useful to his fellow men was his only aim. . . . The hospital has lost in him not only a benefactor, but a strong moral influence whose judgment was sound and wise, whose interest never grew cold, whose word was an asset of unchanging value and the guiding principle of whose life should be the standard in all the affairs of men, pactum serva, keep faith."

Elizabeth Allen Sinkler Coxe died at the age of seventy-six on October 24, 1919, at her home, Windy Hill, in Drifton, Pennsylvania. Her obituary in the *Public Ledger* stated: "The death on Friday last of Mrs. Charles Brinton Coxe at Windy Hill, her beautiful home on the mountain top overlooking the woodland and valleys and the great coal mines of the Coxe estate at Drifton, closes a life of unusual experiences and full of the truest sympathies and greatest charity.... Mrs. Coxe grew up during the Civil War on the family plantation at Belvidere in South Carolina. In a volume privately printed she gives a wonderful picture of what the Civil War, including Sherman's March to the Sea, meant to those who actually lived in and through its darkest hours. Mrs. Coxe wrote with great charm and power of description; but with such simplicity and freedom from any purpose of seeking credit or praise for conduct under most difficult and very trying conditions that the book is worthy of general publication, which she would not permit.... Mrs. Coxe always retained a residence at Drifton during her widowhood, where her son became a most useful citizen, filling positions on the boards of the Hazleton Hospital, the Mining and Mechanical Institute and in the Episcopal church of that diocese. Though living many months of the year in Luzerne county, the mother and son maintained a very hospitable home in Philadelphia. As President of the University Museum the son had supported the scientific work of that body with zeal and great generosity. His expeditions for Egyptian excavations are still being prosecuted under his liberal provisions and his mother has been a warm friend of the museum. Her generous gifts were made to unnumbered worthy objects and institutions and she rarely omitted to meet any appeal. These are some of the reasons for a public interest in the life of Mrs. Coxe. To her very large number of friends and relatives she was endeared by her lovely character and unfailing interest in all that concerned them. Devoted to music she from the first supported the orchestra and opera and during this world war her home was open to many men and women of distinction who came to advocate the claims of the suffering countries of the Allies. ... She was so full of appreciation of what was good and beautiful in life and her extended travels and wide intercourse in the Southern states and at home as well as in Europe and her bright animated nature prevented her ever appearing to grow old.

"She can only be remembered as the most genial, cheerful and responsive of women. Her life has been indeed a boon to all by whom she has been surrounded in every walk of life. Having had many great and harrowing griefs in her own life, she knew what sympathy could do to those whom she aided in every way, as well as to those near and dear to her."

Lizzie was a lady of the American Victorian era. She believed in a panoply of Victorian icons. Her faith was sustained by a belief in an all-powerful, benign God. Relativism was an unknown concept. Her world was ruled by deities that included a belief in absolute truth, an ultimate and ideal good. Her smaller universe was dominated by the desire to do good for her extended family and for her beloved Eckley. She was aware that her South was mired in the aftermath, bitterness, and parochialism produced by the Civil War. She marshaled her resources to help Em, Anne, Liz, and Laura rise above this. She came to maturity before the Civil War. She lived as many of that era, between North and South, knowing both intimately. She had friends and family in both regions. Her life continued after the Civil War not as if a gulf had divided it, but as though there had been a small breach that could be healed. She focused her energies and attention to the new and expanding world of opportunities made possible by her marriage to Charles Coxe, whose family had deep roots in the Industrial Revolution. She welcomed the global closeness made possible by steam, and she embraced the advent of the locomobile (a type of steam car). She was a paragon of the world that was irretrievably lost during the Great War. She was inspired by the past, by Ancient Egypt, and by the Old World of Europe. She nurtured her agrarian Southern roots. She was a lady of deep contrasts, of the South and of the North, of the old and of the new.

Suggested Reading

Allen, Grant. *Paris.* New York: A. Wessels Company, 1904.

Atil, Esin. *Turkish Art.* New York: Harry Abrams, 1980.

Auchincloss, Louis. *The Vanderbilt Era: Profiles of a Gilded Age.* New York: Charles Scribner's Sons, 1989.

Baedeker, Karl. *Egypt and The Sudan.* Leipzig: Karl Baedeker, 1908.

———. *Northern Italy.* Leipzig: Karl Baedeker, 1913.

Baines, John, and Jaromir Malek. *Atlas of Ancient Egypt.* New York: Facts on File, 1980.

Baldwin, William P. *Plantations of the Low Country South Carolina 1697–1865.* Greensboro, S.C.: Legacy, 1985.

Ball, W. Moultrie. *Lt. Colonel Julius Theodore Porcher and Captain John Stoney Porcher of the 10th South Carolina Regiment, Confederate States Army.* Unpublished 107-page typewritten document, in Anne Sinkler Whaley LeClercq's possession, n.d.

Barthorp, Michael. *War on the Nile: Britain, Egypt and the Sudan, 1882–1898.* Dorset, Eng.: Blandford Press, 1984.

Biography Resource Center. Farmington Hills, Mich.: Gale Group, 2004. http://galenet.galegroup.com/servlet/BioRC.

Bohning, James J. "Angel of the Anthracite: The Philanthropic Legacy of Sophia Georgina Coxe." *Canal History and Technology Proceedings* (2005): 150–82.

Breasted, James Henry. *A History of Egypt from the Earliest Times to the Persian Conquest.* New York: Charles Scribner's Sons, 1911.

Brown, A. Samler. *Madeira and the Canary Islands.* London: Sampson, Low, Marston and Co., 1894.

Budge, E. A. *The Nile, Notes for Travellers in Egypt and in the Egyptian Sudan.* London: Thomas Cook and Son, 1910.

Bunson, Margaret. *The Encyclopedia of Ancient Egypt.* New York: Facts on File, 1990.

Burr, Anna Robeson. *Weir Mitchell: His Life and Letters.* New York: Duffield, 1929.

Cadwalader, Sophia H., ed. *Recollections of Joshua Francis Fisher Written in 1864.* Boston: D. B. Updike, Merrymount Press, 1929.

Clark, Thomas D., ed. *South Carolina: The Grand Tour 1780–1865.* Columbia, SC: University of South Carolina Press, 1973.

Cooke, Jacob E. "Tench Coxe, Alexander Hamilton, and the Encouragement of American Manufactures." *William and Mary Quarterly* 32 (1975): 369–92.

Coufopoulos, Demetrius. *A Guide to Constantinople.* London: Adam and Charles Black, 1899.

Cowles, Virginia. *The Kaiser.* New York: Harper & Row, 1963.

Dictionary of National Biography. New York: Oxford University Press, 1999.

Drower, Margaret, ed. *Letters from the Desert: The Correspondence of Flinders and Hilda Petrie.* Oxford: Aris and Phillips, 2004.

Egypt Eyewitness Travel Guide. London: Dorling Kindersley, 2001.

Fishburne, Anne Sinkler. *Belvidere: A Plantation Memory.* Columbia: University of South Carolina Press, 1950.

Harris, George W. *The Practical Guide to Algiers.* London: George Philip & Son, 1899.

Harrison, Eliza Cope. *Best Companions: Letters of Eliza Middleton Fisher and Her Mother, Mary Hering Middleton, from Charleston, Philadelphia, and Newport, 1839–1846.* Columbia: University of South Carolina Press, 2001.

Hichens, Robert. *Egypt and its Monuments.* New York: Century, 1908.

———. *The Near East, Dalmatia, Greece, and Constantinople.* New York: Century, 1913.

Irving, John B. *The South Carolina Jockey Club.* Charleston: Russell & Jones, 1857. Reprint, Spartanburg, SC: Reprint Company, 1975.

Istanbul, the Bosphorus and the Dardanelles. New York: Alfred A. Knopf, 1993.

Jacobs, Sophia Yarnall. *The Clark Inheritance.* New York: Walker, 1981.

Lamplough, A. O. *Egypt and How to See It.* New York: Doubleday, Page, 1907.

Marden, Philip Sanford. *Greece and the Aegean Islands.* Boston: Houghton Mifflin, 1907.

McCoan, J. A. *Egypt.* New York: Peter Fenelon Collier, 1898.

Monmarche, Marcel. *The Chateaux of the Loire.* London: Hachette, 1909.

Newton, Verne W. *The Cambridge Spies: The Untold Story of Maclean, Philby, and Burgess in America.* New York: Madison, 1991.

O'Connor, David, and David Silverman. "The University Museum in Egypt." *Expedition* 21, no. 2 (1979) 4–33.

Piale, Luigi. *Hand-book or New Guide to Naples, Sicily, and the Environs.* Rome: L. Piale, 1853.

Playfair, R. Lambert. *Handbook For Travellers in Algeria and Tunis.* London: John Murray, 1895.

Reynolds-Ball, E. A. *Cairo of To-Day: A Practical Guide to Cairo and its Environs.* London: Adam and Charles Black, 1899.

Richardson, Elizabeth Sinkler. *Recollections.* Unpublished, typewritten document in the possession of author LeClercq, n.d.

Richardson, Rufus B. *Vacation Days in Greece.* New York: Charles Scribner's Sons, 1903.

The Rocks Church Cemetery Burial List. http://www.rootsweb.com/~scbchs/cemlist .htm. Accessed 26 Mar 2004.

Sinkler, Louise E. *Leaves Folded Down.* Wayne, Pa.: Haverford House, 1971.

Slatin, Rudolf Carl, Freiherr von. *Fire and Sword in the Sudan: A Personal Narrative of Fighting and Serving the Dervishes, 1879–1895.* Translated by F. R. Wingate. London: Edward Arnold, 1896.

Swanton, John R. *The Indian Tribes of North America.* Washington: U. S. Government Printing Office, 1953.

Thomas, Nancy, ed. *The American Discovery of Ancient Egypt.* New York: Los Angeles County Museum of Art, 1996.

Van Millingen, Alexander, and Warwick Goble. *Constantinople.* London: A & C. Black, 1906.

Weller, Charles Heald. *Athens and Its Monuments.* New York: Macmillan, 1913.

Wiley, Bell Irvin. *Southern Negroes, 1861–1865.* Baton Rouge: Louisiana State University Press, 1938, 1974.

Wittenberg, Eric J. *The Union Cavalry Comes of Age: Hartwood Church to Brandy Station, 1863.* Washington, D.C.: Brassey's, 2003.

Index

About the Author

A native of Charleston, ANNE SINKLER WHALEY LECLERCQ is the director of the Daniel Library at the Citadel. She holds a master's degree in librarianship from Emory University and a J.D. from the University of Tennessee. LeClercq has written and edited three works drawn from family records: *An Antebellum Plantation Household: Including the South Carolina Low Country Receipts and Remedies of Emily Wharton Sinkler; Between North and South: The Letters of Emily Wharton Sinkler, 1842–1865;* and *Elizabeth Sinkler Coxe's Tales from the Grand Tour, 1890–1910.*